real food
for families

RYLAND
PETERS
& SMALL
LONDON NEW YORK

real food for families

child-friendly food that adults will love too

Fran Warde

photography by Caroline Arber

Dedication

**For my boys, big and little –
David, Otto and Chad.**

First published in the United Kingdom in 2006
by Ryland Peters & Small
20–21 Jockey's Fields
London WC1R 4BW
www.rylandpeters.com

10 9 8 7 6 5 4 3 2 1

Text © Fran Warde 2006
Design and photographs
© Ryland Peters & Small 2006

ISBN-10: 1 84597 217 1
ISBN-13: 978 1 84597 217 2

A CIP catalogue record for this book
is available from the British Library.

Printed and bound in China.

Commissioning Editor Julia Charles
Project Editor Patricia Burgess
Production Sheila Smith
Art Director Anne-Marie Bulat
Publishing Director Alison Starling

Food Stylists Lucy McKelvie, Anna Burges-
Lumsden, Alice Hart and Joss Herd
Prop Stylist Clare Hunt
Indexer Hilary Bird

Notes

• All spoon measurements are level unless
otherwise stated.

• Eggs are UK medium size unless otherwise
specified. Uncooked or partially cooked eggs
should not be served to the very old, frail, young
children, pregnant women or those with
compromised immune systems.

• Ovens should be preheated to the specified
temperature. If using a fan-assisted oven, cooking
times should be adjusted according to the
manufacturer's instructions.

• Health specialists recommend that children
whose families have a history of allergies should
not be given nuts to eat in any form until they are at
least three years old. Children under five should not
be given whole nuts in case of choking.

Author's acknowledgements

Thanks go to my parents for giving me such a
good food start in life. My granny by the sea taught
my mum to cook, my dad bought a lovely house
with a big garden for growing vegetables, and
together as a family of six we all ate freshly
prepared food round the table. It was beautiful
and that simple!

Many thanks to Alison Starling at Ryland Peters &
Small, and special thanks to Julia Charles, who has
a voice that sounds like sunshine on the phone.

Finally, a big thank you to Caroline Arber for her
lovely food photography.

contents

introduction

Nothing is more important than a happy
family, and one way of helping to achieve this is
by providing healthy food. Well-fed children are
bright, funny and good company, and this has
a lot to do with what you feed them. My mantra
is 'cook from scratch'. Convenience foods might
do no long-term harm if used just now and

again, but I'm convinced that too many people have become reliant on them and are jeopardizing their health in the process. Who wants all the fat, sugar and salt they're crammed with? Not me – and I certainly don't want it for my family.

Growing children need a healthy, balanced diet, and they need to be part of making the choices that achieve this. So go shopping together and let them help choose the fruit, vegetables, meat and fish to put in the trolley. Play games while shopping, asking them which country various items come from, whether they grow on trees or in the earth, how they can be cooked, and so forth. They can become

really fascinated by ingredients and keen to discover what they taste like. Children who have seen ingredients in their raw state are not suspicious and confused by a new vegetable that is put in front of them: instead, they feel knowledgeable.

When you're back at home, get them to help unload the shopping and put it away. Filling the fruit bowl, for example, will make them aware of what's available at different times of the year, while stocking dry goods in the larder will alert them to the wealth of ingredients that go into their meals. Then chat about what's for dinner and ask if they'd like to help with the cooking. Perhaps they could wash the potatoes that are going to be baked, or trim the broccoli. While you're working together you could explore their senses, asking if they can name different foods that are salty, sweet, sour or spicy. Start simply and they will let you know if they want to be more involved.

Children are great at laying the table, and enjoy having their particular areas of expertise. For example, I've noticed that little girls seem to love folding napkins and making place cards when two or more families are at the table, while boys enjoy sorting out the glasses and drinks. Everyone has a part to play in healthy family eating, and it's so rewarding to sit around a table chatting, laughing and enjoying good home cooking.

I am passionate about good eating habits in people of all ages. Adults too need good nutrition to feel well and function effectively. There's no need to eat a poor and highly processed diet, even if money is tight, and I believe that the recipes in this book prove it. They're full of flavour and colour, packed with nutrients and, of course, absolutely delicious. I hope they will change the way you cook for your family.

the best start

An old saying tells us, 'Breakfast like a king, lunch like a queen, dine like a pauper', and there's a lot of wisdom in that advice. It's all to do with giving the body the right amount of fuel at the appropriate times of day. We all know how distracted and irritable we can get on an empty stomach, and how uncomfortable it is to go to bed on a full one. Children have slightly different needs from those of adults because they are growing, but one thing is undisputed: we all need a good breakfast to start the day.

Lots of people say that they can't face food in the morning, but that's no excuse for not giving the body some nutrition to help it through till lunchtime. Smoothies are quick and easy to make, full of energy-giving ingredients and slip down with no effort. There's a fantastic selection in this chapter, and there are lots of other ideas for light and healthy breakfasts, including fruit compotes, homemade cereals and yoghurt, delicious breads and muffins, and that perennial favourite – eggs. There really is something for everyone in these pages.

Smoothies are a great way to start the day. Packed with fresh fruit, their lovely fresh, clean flavours will gently awaken your taste buds. They are also good when frozen and served as lollies in the summer. In fact, I know one little boy who will not eat fruit, but loves smoothies, so they're a great way of making sure your family gets the benefit of all the healthy nutrients that fruit contains. If you do not already have a juicer, it's worth investing in one because it makes life easier and you can have fun making up your own combinations of favourite fruits and flavourings.

carrot, apple and ginger smoothie

Preparation 8 minutes
Serves 2

5 large carrots, peeled
5 apples, cored
2.5 cm fresh ginger, peeled

The combination of ingredients in this recipe makes it a fantastic pep-up – great to drink for breakfast or when feeling under the weather. Everyone loves it, although children may take a little while to get used to the slightly hot flavour that the ginger adds.

Press all the prepared ingredients through a juicer and serve immediately.

raspberry, kiwi and blueberry smoothie

Preparation 5 minutes
Serves 2

200 g raspberries, fresh or frozen (no need to thaw)
2 kiwis, peeled
200 g blueberries, fresh or frozen
200 ml milk

Experts tell us that blueberries are great brain food, so blast some together with other delicious fruits and make this wickedly coloured smoothie to serve at any time of the day.

Put everything in a blender and blitz until smooth. Adjust the consistency with milk if you wish, and serve straight away.

strawberry and banana smoothie with wheatgerm

Preparation 10 minutes
Serves 2

225 g strawberries, hulled
2 large bananas
350 ml milk
4 tablespoons natural bio yoghurt
20 g wheatgerm

Full of fruity goodness, this delicious smoothie also contains wheatgerm for extra fibre. It always reminds me of the early morning smoothies I used to drink after swimming at Bondi Beach in Australia. In fact, I think the whole idea of smoothies probably originated Down Under.

Put the prepared fruit in a blender with the milk, yoghurt and wheatgerm. Whiz until smooth and drink straight away.

mango lassi

Preparation 10 minutes
Serves 2

1 cardamom pod (optional)
2 mangoes
200 g natural bio yoghurt
100 ml apple juice
1 tablespoon honey
a pinch of nutmeg

Lassi is an Indian drink – a refreshing mixture of yoghurt and water. It can be flavoured in lots of different ways, but cardamom pods are a traditional addition. This drink is often served with curry to cleanse and cool the palate.

Gently crush the cardamom with a pestle and mortar, discard the pod and crush the seeds.

Peel the mango and cut the flesh away from the stone. Put in a blender with the yoghurt, apple juice, honey, nutmeg and cardamom seeds, whiz until smooth and serve.

There's no better way to preserve the lusciousness of fruit than in a compote – and it's so easy to do. You can use any seasonal ripe fruit and it's lovely to have it all year round with muesli, porridge or homemade yoghurt (see pages 21–22). Compote is also great served as a simple and light dessert after a rich meal. Experiment with combinations of your favourite fruits to make your own particular blend.

winter dried fruit pot

Think of Christmas pudding and this recipe will deliver that intense flavour every morning of the year. The longer you leave it to steep, the more the fruits will plump up.

Preparation 5 minutes
Cooking 30 minutes
Serves 6

150 g dried apricots, stoned
150 g dates, stoned
150 g prunes, stoned
150 g sultanas
150 g dried blueberries
60 g molasses sugar

Put all the ingredients in a saucepan, add just enough water to cover, then stir. Bring to the boil and simmer for 30 minutes. Let cool, then transfer to a storage jar with a tight-fitting lid and refrigerate until needed.

rhubarb and plum compote

Girls just love this fruity compote, probably because of its vibrant pink colour, but everyone enjoys its delicious flavours.

Preparation 10 minutes
Cooking 10 minutes
Serves 6

400 g rhubarb, chopped
400 g plums, stoned
2 cm fresh ginger, peeled and thinly sliced
75 g sugar

Put all the ingredients in a saucepan with 75 ml water, cover with a lid and bring to the boil. Lower the heat and simmer for 5 minutes. Leave the lid on and set aside to cool. Transfer to a storage jar with a tight-fitting lid and refrigerate until needed.

apple and pear compote

This simple combination is a great introductory compote for young children. Serve on its own or with warm porridge, or use as the basis of a crumble.

Preparation 10 minutes
Cooking 10 minutes
Serves 6

500 g apples, peeled, cored and chopped
500 g pears, peeled, cored and chopped
60 g light brown sugar
1 vanilla bean, split lengthways

Put the fruit in a saucepan with 50 ml water, then add the sugar and vanilla pod. Stir, cover with a lid and bring to the boil. Lower the heat and simmer for 5 minutes. Leave the lid on and set aside to cool. Transfer to a storage jar with a tight-fitting lid and refrigerate until needed.

Nothing beats a bowl of hot, creamy porridge to get the day off to a good start: it's quick, easy, unprocessed, nutritious and is digested slowly, so it keeps you going until lunchtime. Always soak the oats overnight as this makes for a creamier consistency. If you're in a hurry, you can make porridge in the microwave: cook on full power for about three minutes, then stir and cook for another minute.

muesli

It's great to be in control of what goes in your breakfast cereal, and this recipe allows you to do just that. For a soft and creamy breakfast, combine equal amounts of this muesli with yoghurt and leave to soak overnight.

Preparation 20 minutes
Serves 6

200 g rolled oats
75 g bran flakes
40 g wheatgerm
75 g dried apricots, chopped
75 g dried cherries
75 g sultanas
40 g desiccated coconut
75 g hazelnuts, toasted and chopped
75 g pecans, chopped
25 g sunflower seeds

Put all the ingredients in an airtight container and mix together well.

granola

You'll recognize this cereal as crunchy muesli. It's delicious for breakfast or as a tasty nibble straight from the jar. The more maple syrup you add, the crunchier the mixture will be.

Preparation 20 minutes
Cooking 45 minutes
Serves 4

300 g rolled oats
100 g almonds
30 g pumpkin seeds
30 g sunflower seeds
15 g sesame seeds
250 ml maple syrup
100 g dried apricots
100 g sultanas
20 g powdered milk

Preheat the oven to 170°C (325°F) Gas 3 and line a baking sheet with parchment.

Put the oats, almonds and seeds in a bowl and mix well. Spread on the baking sheet in an even layer and drizzle with the maple syrup. Put in the oven and bake for 25 minutes.

Remove the baking sheet, add the dried fruit and powdered milk and mix well. Return to the oven and bake for a further 15 minutes, until the mixture is crisp and golden. Let cool, then store in an airtight container.

dairy porridge

Packed with goodness, this is great for growing children.

Preparation 5 minutes + overnight soaking
Cooking 8 minutes
Serves 4

125 g rolled oats
1 litre milk

Place the milk and oats in a non-stick saucepan. Stir, cover and leave in a cool place overnight.

The next day bring to the boil, stirring constantly, and simmer for 1 minute. Adjust the consistency with a little more milk if necessary, and serve.

water porridge

This is ideal if you need to lower your dairy intake. You can add a little milk at the table, if you wish.

Preparation 5 minutes + overnight soaking
Cooking 8 minutes
Serves 4

125 g rolled oats

Place the oats and 1 litre water in a non-stick saucepan. Stir, cover with a lid and leave in a cool place overnight.

The next day, bring to the boil, stirring constantly, then simmer for 1 minute. Adjust the consistency with a little more water if necessary, and serve.

Calcium is vital for healthy teeth and bones, and eating yoghurt is a great way of getting enough. Making your own is really easy, and much more nutritious than ready-made, which is often full of added sugar. It is best to make it in a special yoghurt machine according to the manufacturer's instructions, but note that it will be runnier than shop-bought yoghurt, which generally has artificial gums and thickeners added. However, you can make homemade yoghurt thicker if you strain it through muslin.

plum and honey cup

When plums are abundant simmer them and serve with a luscious mixture of yoghurt and mascarpone.

Preparation 10 minutes
Cooking 15 minutes
Serves 4

500 g plums
2 tablespoons honey
200 g natural bio yoghurt
200 g mascarpone

Stone the plums and put in a saucepan with the honey and 50 ml water. Bring to the boil over a medium heat, then cover and simmer very gently for about 8 minutes. Set aside to cool.

Mix the yoghurt and mascarpone together. Half-fill 4 glasses with this, then top with the cooked plums.

frozen berry yoghurt cup

During the winter months bags of frozen berries provide a lovely taste of summer. Layered up with yoghurt, they make a great breakfast or pudding treat.

Preparation 10 minutes
Serves 4

500 g frozen mixed berries
100 g unrefined caster sugar
400 g natural Greek yoghurt

Put the frozen berries in a blender with the sugar and blitz into small pieces. Take 4 glasses and fill with alternating layers of yoghurt and berries. Let sit for 5 minutes before serving.

banana, pecan and granola yoghurt pot

This mixture is always a taste of heaven either for breakfast or at the end of the day.

Preparation 10 minutes
Serves 4

400 g natural bio yoghurt
3 ripe bananas, sliced
50 g pecans
75 g molasses sugar
100 g granola (see page 21)
50 g chocolate, grated

Spoon some yoghurt into 4 glasses. Top with the bananas, then add the pecans, molasses sugar and granola. Spoon the remaining yoghurt over the top, then sprinkle with the chocolate and serve.

It's fantastically relaxing to knead your own dough, but few of us have the time to do so. That's where bread machines come in. They deliver great loaves with very little effort, and you can be certain that they contain none of the undesirable additives found in ready-made bread. Of course, the lack of preservatives means that they don't keep very long, so store the bread in an airtight container or wrapped in the fridge. If you prefer your loaves with a soft crust, put the warm bread in a plastic bag to cool.

wholemeal bread

This is a staple in our house, and a whole loaf can disappear at a single meal. But it doesn't matter, as I just fill the machine again and a little while later another lovely fresh loaf appears.

Preparation 10 minutes
Cooking approx. 3 hours in bread machine
Makes 1 loaf

350 ml warm water
7 g quick yeast
1 tablespoon sugar
¼ teaspoon vitamin C powder
4 tablespoons olive oil
500 g wholemeal flour
½ teaspoon salt

Pour the water into a jug, dissolve the yeast, sugar and vitamin C powder in it and let stand for 5 minutes. Pour the liquid into the bread machine with the oil and add the flour and salt. Switch the machine to the wholemeal setting and bake the mixture according to the manufacturer's instructions.

granary bread

A lovely speckled loaf – delicious with cheese and chutney.

Preparation 10 minutes
Cooking approx. 3 hours in bread machine
Makes 1 loaf

350 ml warm water
7 g quick yeast
1 tablespoon sugar
¼ teaspoon vitamin C powder
4 tablespoons vegetable oil
500 g granary flour
½ teaspoon salt

Pour the water into a jug, dissolve the yeast, sugar and vitamin C powder in it and let stand for 5 minutes. Pour the liquid into the bread machine with the oil and add the flour and salt. Switch the machine to the granary or wholemeal setting and bake according to the manufacturer's instructions.

milky white bread

Slightly richer than an ordinary white loaf, and great for toasting.

Preparation 10 minutes
Cooking approx. 3 hours in bread machine
Makes 1 loaf

350 ml warm milk
7 g quick yeast
1 tablespoon sugar
¼ teaspoon vitamin C powder
500 g strong white flour
½ teaspoon salt

Pour the milk into a jug, dissolve the yeast, sugar and vitamin C powder in it and let stand for 5 minutes. Pour the liquid into the bread machine with the oil and add the flour and salt. Switch the machine to the white bread setting and bake according to the manufacturer's instructions.

These homemade breakfast muffins are full of fibre and goodness instead of the usual load of sugar. They also make tasty lunch box treats. It's worth buying a flexible plastic muffin tin: it does away with the need for fiddly paper cases and produces perfect muffins every time.

oat and apple muffins

Children love helping to make these muffins, and they certainly enjoy eating them.

Preparation 15 minutes
Cooking 30–40 minutes
Makes 6

50 g rolled oats
200 g plain flour
2 teaspoons baking powder
½ teaspoon bicarbonate of soda
100 g golden caster sugar
2 eggs, beaten
100 ml vegetable oil
2 apples, grated

a 6-hole muffin tin, preferably non-stick

Preheat the oven to 180°C (350°F) Gas 4. If necessary, line your muffin tin with paper cases.

Put the oats, flour, baking powder, bicarbonate of soda and sugar in a bowl and mix well. Beat together the eggs and oil and pour into the mixing bowl. Add the grated apple and mix together quickly (overmixing will make the muffins lose their light texture). Spoon the mixture into 6 muffin cases. Sprinkle the top of each with a little extra sugar and bake in the middle of the oven for 30–40 minutes. Test for readiness by inserting a knife: the blade should come out clean. Eat warm or cold.

frozen berry muffins

Spelt is an ancient variety of wheat. Its flour adds texture to these muffins.

Preparation 15 minutes
Cooking 30–40 minutes
Makes 6

225 g spelt flour
2 teaspoons baking powder
½ teaspoon bicarbonate of soda
100 g sugar
2 eggs, beaten
100 ml vegetable oil
160 g frozen berries (no need to thaw)

a 6-hole muffin tin, preferably non-stick

Preheat the oven to 180°C (350°F) Gas 4. If necessary, line your muffin tin with paper cases.

Put the flour, baking powder, bicarbonate of soda and sugar in a bowl and mix well. Beat together the eggs and oil, pour into the mixing bowl, then add the berries. Mix together quickly so that the muffins do not lose their light texture. Spoon into 6 muffin cases and bake in the middle of the oven for 30–40 minutes. Test for readiness by inserting a knife: the blade should come out clean. Eat warm or cold.

wholemeal banana and chocolate muffins

Preparation 20 minutes
Cooking 40 minutes
Makes 6

225 g wholemeal flour
2 teaspoons baking powder
100 g unrefined caster sugar
75 g chocolate drops
2 eggs, beaten
100 ml vegetable oil
2 bananas

a 6-hole muffin tin, preferably non-stick

The chocolate and wholemeal make this a muffin that combines indulgence with virtue. It's also great for using up those overripe bananas in the fruit bowl.

Preheat the oven to 180ºC (350ºF) Gas 4. If necessary, line the muffin tin with paper cases.

Put the flour, baking powder, sugar and chocolate drops in a bowl and mix well. Beat together the eggs and oil and pour into the bowl. Mash the bananas with the back of a fork, add to the bowl and mix together quickly: the mixture will be quite stiff. Take care not to overmix or the muffins will be heavy. Spoon the mixture into the muffin cases and bake in the middle of the oven for 40 minutes. Test for readiness by inserting a knife: the blade should come out clean. Eat warm or cold.

Eggs must surely be one of the most useful and nutritious foods: they're certainly among the most versatile. They are a good source of protein but, unlike many meat and dairy products, they are low in saturated fat and can therefore be eaten up to six times a week. (Only people with a cholesterol problem might want to eat them a bit less often.) I always recommend free-range eggs, but make sure you buy from somewhere with a high turnover so that they're really fresh. When you break them open the yolk should have a good dome and the white should be thinner at the edges than around the yolk.

flat eggs

My two little boys always refer to fried eggs as 'flat eggs', and this is what we and many of our friends now call them. No matter how you know them, they're a healthy way to start the day.

Cooking 1–2 minutes
Serves 4

3 tablespoons olive oil
4 eggs

Heat the oil in a heavy-based frying pan. When hot, add the eggs, cover the pan and cook over a medium heat for 1 minute. When the white is cooked through, lift each egg out with a spatula and serve on toasted granary bread.

boiled eggs

Most of us probably first encountered eggs softly boiled and accompanied by buttered toast 'soldiers' for dipping. There's no improving on this classic.

Cooking 4–6 minutes
Serves 4

4 eggs

Boil a kettle of water and pour into a saucepan on the heat. Carefully lower the eggs into the water, then cover and simmer: 4 minutes for soft yolks, 6 minutes for hard. Remove from the pan with a slotted spoon and serve with toast soldiers.

poached eggs

There's no need to be nervous about poaching eggs in a pan of water, but if you prefer, you can use an egg poacher. The shape is not as relaxed, but they taste just the same.

Cooking 6–8 minutes
Serves 4

4 eggs

Boil a kettle of water and pour into a large saucepan. Crack the eggs into 4 cups, stir the water with a spoon and gently slip each egg into it. Bring to a gentle simmer, then cover with a lid, remove from the heat and let stand: 5 minutes for soft poached eggs, and slightly longer if you prefer the yolk hard. Lift the eggs from the water with a slotted spoon and rest on kitchen paper to remove any excess water. Serve on toast, perhaps with a slice of ham underneath the egg.

omelette

Whether plain or filled with whatever you happen to have in the fridge, omelettes are a great standby meal. My boys and I often make a large one and cut it into portions, which means we can all eat at the same time.

Preparation 5 minutes
Cooking 5 minutes
Serves 3

6 eggs
6 tablespoons milk
50 g butter
sea salt and freshly ground black pepper

Whisk together the eggs, milk and seasoning. Melt the butter in a large non-stick frying pan, then pour in the egg mixture, using a fork to lift the set egg and let the liquid egg flow underneath. Cook until the top is just soft. Using a palette knife, fold over one-third of the omelette, then turn out and fold over again. Cut into portions and serve at the table.

eggs cocotte

These baked eggs go down a treat at breakfast, or as a light meal when time is short.

Preparation 10 minutes
Cooking 6 minutes
Serves 4

60 g fresh spinach, chopped
4 eggs
4 tablespoons milk
75 g Parmesan cheese, grated
sea salt and freshly ground black pepper

4 ovenproof ramekins, buttered

Preheat the oven to 200°C (400°F) Gas 6. Divide the spinach between the prepared ramekins. Crack an egg on top, add a spoonful of milk to each, then season and top with the Parmesan. Place the ramekins on a baking sheet in the preheated oven and cook for 6 minutes.

scrambled eggs

There are two ways of cooking scrambled eggs:
in the microwave or on the hob in a non-stick pan.
I prefer the second method because it allows you
to stir the eggs to creamy perfection.

Preparation 2 minutes
Cooking 3 minutes
Serves 2–3

6 eggs
4 tablespoons milk
30 g butter
sea salt and freshly ground black pepper
choped chives, to serve

Whisk the eggs together with the milk and seasoning.
Melt the butter in a medium non-stick pan, then add the
egg mixture, stirring frequently until it reaches a creamy
consistency. Serve with a sprinkling of chopped chives
and hot buttered toast. For a real treat add a few slices
of smoked salmon.

family lunch boxes

I am a great fan of packed lunches because I know exactly what my children are eating. When they get in from school I can see what's left and we can have a chat about it so that I can try to give them other healthy alternatives.

Forget soggy sandwiches, limp biscuits and fatty crisps. Think instead of crunchy salads, light ciabatta rolls filled with hoummus, Parma ham and cucumber, noodles with shredded chicken, pesto and Parmesan pasta, tortillas, muffins... the possibilities are endless. When time is short do not be afraid of buying a good-quality sausage roll and putting it in a box with carrot sticks, cucumber and a few crisp lettuce leaves. Every so often it's necessary to compromise – even in my kitchen!

Don't forget that the grown-ups in the family also deserve a healthy lunch, so invest in some good lunch boxes that do not leak, and buy small vacuum flasks for colder months, when you can fill them with hearty soups.

spicy vegetable wrap

Preparation 10 minutes
Serves 4

4 flat breads
harissa (optional)
2 carrots, grated
1 courgette, grated
2 spring onions, finely chopped
75 g sun-blushed tomatoes
8 iceberg leaves, chopped

The spice in this wrap comes from harissa, a red Moroccan paste (see page 117). If your family isn't keen on spicy food, simply leave it out or replace it with Marmite.

Spread the flat breads with harissa, if using, leaving a 2-cm border around the edge. Sprinkle with a layer of grated carrot, then layers of courgette, spring onions, tomatoes and lettuce.

Roll the flat bread up tightly into a cigar shape. Cut in half across the middle, wrap in clingfilm and pop in the lunch box.

ham and cheese flat bread

Preparation 5 minutes
Cooking 10 minutes
Serves 4

8 x 18 cm flat breads
8 slices air-dried ham, such as Parma or Bayonne
8 slices Gruyère, Emmental or other hard cheese
sea salt and freshly ground black pepper
olive oil, for frying

This is something like an instant pizza. While great for lunch boxes, it's also good cut into small pieces and served with drinks.

Lay out four of the flat breads and cover each with 2 slices of ham and 2 slices of cheese. Season and top with the remaining breads.

Heat a frying pan large enough to hold one whole flat-bread sandwich. Brush with a little olive oil and fry for 2–3 minutes on each side, until golden. Repeat with the remaining sandwiches. Cut into wedges and serve hot or cold.

classic smoked salmon bagel

Preparation 10 minutes
Serves 4

4 bagels
80 g cream cheese
½ cucumber, sliced
200 g smoked salmon
½ lemon
sea salt and freshly ground black pepper

This is an elegant way of adding fish oils to your diet – and it couldn't be more delicious

Cut the bagels in half and spread with the cream cheese. Top with some cucumber and slivers of smoked salmon, season and squeeze a little lemon juice over. Sandwich together and enjoy!

carrot, chicken and toasted sesame pouch

Preparation 10 minutes
Serves 4

4 pita breads
4 carrots, grated
200 g cooked chicken, cut into thin strips
20 g sesame seeds, toasted
1 tablespoon sesame oil
sea salt and freshly ground black pepper

Pack tasty ingredients into a pita bread and you have a great transportable meal. The grated carrot makes it lovely and moist.

Toast the pita breads and slit open to cool. Put the carrot in a bowl with the chicken, add the sesame seeds, oil and seasoning and mix well. Generously fill the pouches and wrap in clingfilm.

Think of dips and most of us usually think of parties – but they're so light and delicious that they deserve to be eaten on other occasions too. In fact, they're terrific portable food, so they're ideal for lunch boxes. Serve them with a colourful selection of crudités, some breadsticks or crackers and you have a healthy lunch that's high in lots of essential vitamins and minerals.

guacamole

Preparation 15 minutes
Serves 4–6

Juice of 1 lemon
3 spring onions, thinly sliced
3 tomatoes, peeled, deseeded and chopped
1 chilli, finely diced
1 garlic clove, finely chopped
2 ripe avocados
a bunch of coriander, chopped
2 tablespoons olive oil
sea salt and freshly ground black pepper

Although avocados are high in fat, they are also full of other valuable nutrients. The lovely colour will entice the most reluctant eater.

Put the lemon juice in a mixing bowl with the spring onions, tomatoes, chilli and garlic. Peel and finely dice the avocado, add to the bowl and mix well. Add the coriander, olive oil and seasoning and mix well. Serve with taco chips or crunchy vegetable sticks.

harissa and herb dip

Preparation 20 minutes
Cooking 50 minutes
Serves 4–6

1 quantity harissa (see page 117)
a bunch of coriander, finely chopped
a bunch of flat leaf parsley, finely chopped

This lovely dip has a warming spiciness that makes it irresistible. Keep a jar of it in the fridge to spice up sandwiches.

Make the harissa as described on page 117. When cool, stir in the coriander and parsley and serve with baked fish, barbecued chicken or lamb. It can also be stirred through new potatoes, rice or chickpeas.

lemony hoummus

Preparation 10 minutes + overnight
soaking
Cooking 1 hour 30 minutes
Serves 4

125 g dried chickpeas
1 tablespoon tahini
75 ml olive oil
juice of ½ lemon
2 garlic cloves, crushed
sea salt and freshly ground black pepper

The flavour of this hoummus is fresh and delicious –
so different from ready-made that it might take a little
time for some family members to be converted. Rest
assured, they will come round...

Put the chickpeas in a bowl, cover generously with cold water
and let soak for 12 hours. Drain, transfer to a small saucepan
and cover with fresh water. Bring to the boil and allow to
bubble furiously for 10 minutes. Lower the heat and simmer
for 1½ hours, until soft. Add more water if needed. Drain and
reserve the cooking water.

Put the chickpeas in a food processor. Add the tahini, olive
oil, lemon juice, garlic and 75 ml of the reserved water.
Season and blend until smooth and creamy. Adjust the
consistency if you wish by adding more of the cooking water.
(You cannot overblend this: it just gets better.) Serve with
vegetable sticks or warm pita bread to dip.

cheese dip

Preparation 5 minutes
Serves 4

150 g soft blue cheese, such as St Agur
75 g cream cheese
1 tablespoon olive oil

This tasty dip is naughty on the hips, but simple to
make and truly delicious!

Put the two cheeses in a bowl and mash with a fork. Transfer
to a serving bowl and drizzle with the olive oil. Serve with
cheese biscuits, toasted wholemeal bread or vegetable sticks.

tzatziki

Preparation 10 minutes + 45 minutes
for straining
Serves 4

1 cucumber, grated
a bunch of mint, chopped
2 garlic cloves, crushed
300 g Greek yoghurt
sea salt and freshly ground black pepper

The clean flavours of this Greek dip make it really
refreshing on a summer's day.

Put the cucumber in a sieve over a bowl and leave for
45 minutes, until the excess liquid has dripped out. Mix
the remaining ingredients together, then season and add
the cucumber. Stir well and serve with toasted pita bread
and vegetable sticks.

oven-roasted vegetables with chickpeas and couscous

Preparation 30 minutes

Cooking 40 minutes

Serves 4

2 tablespoons olive oil

2 garlic cloves, chopped

1 teaspoon sweet paprika

2 red onions, cut into wedges

1 large red pepper, deseeded and sliced

1 small butternut squash, unpeeled, cut into wedges

200 g cherry or baby plum tomatoes

100 g green beans, trimmed

2 sprigs of fresh thyme

200 g couscous

1 x 240-g can chickpeas, drained

finely grated zest and juice of 1 unwaxed lemon

sea salt and freshly ground black pepper

Give vegetables a new lease of life by roasting them until they are deliciously caramelized and serving them with no-cook couscous.

Preheat the oven to 200°C (400°F) Gas 6. Lightly oil a large roasting tin.

Pour the olive oil into a large bowl and add the garlic and paprika. Season well and mix. Place the prepared vegetables in the bowl along with the tomatoes and green beans. Stir until they are well coated with the flavoured oil.

Put the vegetables in the prepared roasting tin with the sprigs of thyme. Cook in the oven for 20 minutes, moving them around at intervals (using a large metal spoon) to ensure even roasting. Reduce the heat to 180°C (350°F) Gas 4 and roast for a further 20 minutes.

Put the couscous in a large bowl and add 275 ml of hot water, stir well, cover and let stand for 5–10 minutes. Meanwhile, put the chickpeas in a saucepan of boiling water and allow them to boil for 2 minutes. Drain and add the chickpeas to the couscous, mixing well to fluff up the couscous. Add the roasted vegetables.

Put 4 tablespoons hot water into the roasting tin and mix well to combine with the vegetable juices. Spoon this mixture over the vegetables and couscous. Add the lemon juice and zest and fold everything together. Spoon individual portions into airtight containers and store in the fridge until needed.

lentil and baked tomato salad

Preparation 10 minutes
Cooking 50 minutes
Serves 4

300 g dried Puy lentils
250 g cherry tomatoes
80 g stoned olives
75 g Parmesan cheese
2 tablespoons balsamic vinegar
sea salt and freshly ground black pepper
olive oil, for baking and dressing

Puy lentils are a must for this recipe as they do not collapse when cooked. They give this salad fantastic flavour and texture.

Put the lentils in a saucepan, cover with water and bring to the boil. Lower the heat and simmer for 40 minutes, until soft.

Preheat the oven to 130°C (250°F) Gas 1. Put the tomatoes on a non-stick baking sheet, drizzle 3 tabespoons of olive oil over them, then put in the oven and bake for 40 minutes.

Drain the lentils when cooked and put in a serving bowl. Add the tomatoes, olives and seasoning. Grate the Parmesan over the top and drizzle with olive oil and balsamic vinegar. Lightly mix and serve.

kidney bean, egg and ham salad

Preparation 20 minutes
+ overnight soaking
Cooking 1 hour 40 minutes
Serves 4

175 g dried kidney beans
2 Baby Gem lettuces
200 g cooked ham, chopped
4 hard-boiled eggs, quartered
a bunch of freshly chopped parsley
Dressing
1 teaspoon Dijon mustard
1 teaspoon runny honey
1 tablespoon red wine vinegar
1 garlic clove, crushed
½ teaspoon unrefined caster sugar
3 tablespoons olive oil
sea salt and freshly ground black pepper

The joy of this salad is that it contains a generous amount of essential nutrients – and it tastes great!

Soak the beans in a large bowl of water overnight. Drain and transfer to a saucepan, cover with water and bring to the boil. Allow to bubble furiously for 10 minutes, then simmer for 1 hour 20 minutes, until soft. Add more water while cooking, if needed, then drain, rinse and cool.

Separate the lettuce leaves and use to line a salad bowl. Add the kidney beans, ham and eggs. Whisk together the dressing ingredients, then pour over the salad and sprinkle with the parsley. Toss before serving.

thai chicken noodle salad

Most people love noodles, and the delicate spiciness in this recipe should not overpower sensitive taste buds. However, you can deseed the chillies if you prefer a milder flavour.

Preparation 20 minutes
Cooking 10 minutes
Serves 4

1 tablespoon vegetable oil
350 g chicken breast, thinly sliced
1 cm fresh ginger, peeled and chopped
2 garlic cloves, crushed
1 lemongrass stick, thinly sliced
1 medium-hot red or green chilli, finely diced
300 g thick noodles
100 g pak choi, chopped
1 lime, to serve

Heat the oil in a wok or large frying pan, add the chicken, ginger, garlic, lemongrass and chilli, stir well and cook on a medium heat for 5 minutes.

Meanwhile, cook the noodles according to the packet instructions, then drain.

Add the pak choi and cooked noodles to the wok and toss well. Serve with wedges of lime.

ginger vegetable noodles

Even reluctant vegetable eaters will enjoy this. Its glorious colours are hard to resist.

Preparation 20 minutes
Cooking 10 minutes
Serves 4

300 g noodles
2 tablespoons sesame oil
5 cm fresh ginger, peeled and chopped
2 garlic cloves, crushed
2 teaspoons miso paste
100 g green beans, trimmed
100 g mangetout, trimmed
100 g small asparagus, trimmed
100 g baby sweetcorn, trimmed
200 g beansprouts
1 tablespoon soy sauce
1 teaspoon sugar
a bunch of fresh coriander, chopped
4 spring onions, thinly sliced

Cook the noodles according to the packet instructions. Drain and toss in 1 tablespoon of sesame oil to stop them sticking together. Set aside.

Heat a tablespoon of oil in a wok or large frying pan, add the ginger and garlic and cook briefly without browning. Add the miso paste and 150 ml water and simmer for 5 minutes. Stir in the green beans, mangetout, asparagus and sweetcorn and cook for 2 minutes. Add the beansprouts, soy sauce, sugar and noodles, toss well, then transfer to a flask and seal. Put the coriander and spring onions in a small pot to add just before eating.

rice noodle salad with prawns

A delicious and sustaining lunch. If you'd like to spice it up a little more for adults, add some chopped spring onions, fresh coriander and red chilli.

Preparation 15 minutes
Cooking 10 minutes
Serves 6

150 g thin rice noodles
2 tablespoons vegetable oil
1 cm fresh ginger, peeled and chopped
1 garlic clove, chopped
175 g cooked peeled prawns
50 g fine green beans, trimmed
1 carrot, cut into matchsticks
juice of $\frac{1}{2}$ a lime
50 g cashew nuts, chopped
1 tablespoon sesame seeds, toasted

Cook the noodles according to the packet instructions. Drain, toss them in a little of the oil and let cool in the colander for 10 minutes.

Heat the remaining oil in a wok or large frying pan and add the ginger, garlic, prawns, beans and carrot. Cook over a medium heat for 4 minutes, stirring constantly. Add the mixture to the cooled noodles and mix well. Spoon individual portions into airtight containers and sprinkle with cashew nuts and toasted sesame seeds.

parmesan and ham straws

Cheese straws are great 'mobile food'. Serve them in lunch boxes or at drinks parties.

Preparation 30 minutes
Cooking 30 minutes
Makes 12–15

500 g ready-made puff pastry
1 egg, beaten
100 g Parmesan or other hard cheese, grated
4 slices Parma ham

Preheat the oven to 180ºC (350ºF) Gas 4. Lightly dust a work surface with flour and roll out the pastry to approximately 30 x 30 cm. Brush all over with half of the beaten egg. Cut the pastry in half and sprinkle one half with 75 g of the cheese. Cover with the Parma ham and place the remaining pastry on top. Roll firmly together into a rectangle about 20 x 20 cm. Cut into strips 2.5 cm wide, then carefully twist each one about 3 or 4 times.

Place the straws on a baking sheet, brush with the remaining egg and sprinkle with the remaining cheese. Bake for 30 minutes, until puffed and golden.

real sausage rolls

Abandon the usual bland sausage-meat and use good-quality sausages for these top-notch rolls.

Preparation 20 minutes
Cooking 45 minutes
Makes 6

500 g ready-made puff pastry
1 egg, beaten
6 good-quality sausages
flour, for dusting

Preheat the oven to 180°C (350°F) Gas 4. Dust a work surface with flour and roll out the pastry to approximately 30 x 30 cm. Cut the pastry into three strips just smaller in width than the sausages. Brush all over with beaten egg. Place a sausage at the end of one strip and roll up, using half the strip. Cut the pastry, pat it firmly around the sausage, then place seam-side down on a baking sheet. Repeat this process with the remaining sausages.

Brush each roll with beaten egg and make a few small slashes in the top with a sharp knife. Transfer to the middle of the oven and bake for 30 minutes, then reduce the heat to 150°C (300°F) Gas 2 and cook for a further 15 minutes. Serve hot or cold.

chorizo and bean pasties

If you've never had chorizo, you're in for a treat. It's a Spanish sausage, available in various degrees of spiciness, and is just delicious.

Preparation 30 minutes
Cooking 40 minutes
Makes 4

200 g haricot beans, cooked and drained
150 g chorizo, chopped
50 g Manchego or other hard cheese, grated
1 tablespoon plain flour
500 g ready-made puff pastry
1 egg, beaten
sea salt and freshly ground black pepper

Preheat the oven to 180ºC (350ºF) Gas 4, then lightly oil a baking sheet.

Put the haricot beans in a bowl, add the chorizo, cheese and flour, season and mix well. Pour in 50 ml water and stir again.

Lightly dust a work surface with flour, then roll out the pastry to approximately 30 x 30 cm. Cut the pastry into 4 equal squares and spoon the chorizo mixture into the middle of each one. Brush the edges with beaten egg, then fold two opposite corners together to make a triangular shape. Press all round the edges to seal.

Place the pasties on a baking sheet and brush the tops with beaten egg. Make a small slash in the top of each pasty, then bake in the middle of the oven for 40 minutes. These savouries can be eaten hot or cold.

chicken soup

Preparation 20 minutes
Cooking 40 minutes
Serves 4

1 tablespoon olive oil
1 onion, chopped
1 garlic clove, crushed
2 chicken breasts, diced
2 leeks, chopped
200 g potatoes, unpeeled and chopped
1.2 litres chicken stock
3 sprigs of thyme
2 bay leaves
kernels from 1 cob of sweetcorn
sea salt and freshly ground black pepper

A bowlful of this comforting soup makes everyone feel better, especially when served with warm homemade bread (see page 25).

Heat the olive oil in a saucepan, add the onion, garlic, chicken and leeks and sauté gently for 8 minutes without browning. Add the potatoes, stock, thyme and bay leaves, then season and simmer for 20 minutes.

Add the sweetcorn kernels and cook for a further 10 minutes. Remove the thyme and bay leaves before serving.

pea and ham soup

Preparation 15 minutes
Cooking 40 minutes
Serves 4

2 tablespoons olive oil
1 onion, chopped
250 g cooked ham, chopped
1.2 litres vegetable or ham stock
350 g peas, fresh or frozen
(no need to thaw)
sea salt and freshly ground black pepper

Easy to make and hearty enough for the coldest winter's day. People of all ages love this soup.

Heat the oil in a saucepan, add the onion and sauté for 5 minutes without browning. Add the ham, then pour in the stock and bring to the boil. Lower the heat and simmer for 25 minutes.

Add the peas and some seasoning and cook for a further 5 minutes. (Frozen peas should be cooked for a little longer.) Transfer the soup to a blender or food processor and blitz until smooth. Adjust the consistency if you wish by adding a little more stock or water, and serve topped with a drizzle of olive oil.

quick weekday suppers

Busy days spent working or dashing around after the children can leave you weary and dreading the thought of preparing the evening meal. This needn't be the case if you ensure you always have a stock of basic ingredients and you have some easy recipes up your sleeve that you feel confident about cooking. The ideas in the following pages all fit that bill.

In many families eating together has become something of a lost tradition, or it's done in front of the television, and I think that's a real pity. Mealtimes are a great opportunity for relaxing and sharing news and ideas: they really do bring the family closer together. If you and yours have lost the habit of sitting round the dinner table, try to make it a rule that you all eat together at least once a week. On days when you all have different commitments and it's just not possible, make a dish that lends itself to being kept warm or reheated so that people can help themselves as they come and go. Ideal dishes include Italian meatballs, three-cheese cauliflower, Lancashire hotpot and easy tuna fish cakes, all served with mashed potato (which won't spoil).

chicken and broccoli noodles

Preparation 10 minutes
Cooking 15 minutes
Serves 4

300 g egg noodles
1 tablespoon vegetable oil
3 chicken breasts, cut into strips
200 g broccoli florets
1 garlic clove, crushed
1 red chilli, diced (optional)
50 g sesame seeds, toasted
75 g cashew nuts
1 tablespoon sesame oil
soy sauce, to serve

Tasty, satisfying and healthy – what more could you want from a quick weekday supper?

Cook the noodles according to the packet instructions, then drain and set aside.

Heat the oil in a large pan, add the chicken and cook over a high heat for 5 minutes, until golden. Stir in the broccoli and cook for 2 minutes. Add the garlic, chilli and sesame seeds and cook for 2 more minutes. Add the noodles, toss well and cook for a further 3 minutes. Finally, add the cashews and sesame oil, stir through the mixture and serve with soy sauce at the table.

pasta with ham and peas

Preparation 10 minutes
Cooking 10 minutes
Serves 4

300 g pasta
1 tablespoon olive oil
1 shallot, diced
1 garlic clove, crushed
200 g cooked ham, chopped
200 g peas, fresh or frozen
(no need to thaw)
100 ml double cream
2 egg yolks
75 g Parmesan cheese, grated
sea salt and freshly ground black pepper

This classic Italian recipe gives a new twist to ham and eggs.

Bring a large pan of salted water to the boil, add the pasta and cook according to the packet instructions. Drain and return it to the pan.

Meanwhile, heat the oil in a saucepan, add the shallot and garlic and sauté over a low heat until soft.

Put the ham, peas and cream in another pan and heat to a gentle simmer. Remove from the heat and add the egg yolks, Parmesan and seasoning. Mix well so that the egg does not scramble. Finally, add the sautéd garlic and shallot, toss through the pasta and serve.

italian meatballs with pasta

Preparation 30 minutes
Cooking 1 hour
Serves 4

4 tablespoons olive oil
2 onions, finely chopped
2 garlic cloves, finely chopped
700 g tomato passata
100 ml red wine
1 bay leaf and 2 sprigs of thyme
250 g minced pork
250 g minced beef
a bunch of flat leaf parsley, chopped
1 egg
300 g spaghetti
sea salt and freshly ground black pepper
freshly grated Parmesan cheese, to serve

Offer this with a bowl of dried chilli flakes so that people can spice it up if they like.

Heat half the oil in a frying pan, add half the onion and garlic, and sauté gently for 5 minutes. Add the passata, wine, bay leaf, thyme and seasoning, and simmer gently for 30 minutes.

Put the remaining onion and garlic in a large bowl, add the pork, beef, parsley, egg and seasoning and combine thoroughly. Divide into 16 equal pieces and shape into balls. Heat the remaining oil in a large pan and brown the meatballs all over. Pour the sauce into the pan, then cover and simmer for 20 minutes.

Meanwhile, cook the spaghetti according to the packet instructions. Serve topped with the meatballs and grated Parmesan cheese.

sausage and bacon toad-in-the-hole

Preparation 20 minutes
+ 30 minutes resting

Cooking 35 minutes

Serves 4–6

175 g flour

2 eggs

150 ml milk

150 ml water

8 slices streaky bacon

800 g sausages

2 red onions, cut into wedges

sea salt and freshly ground black pepper

A fun Friday night supper that everyone enjoys – especially with a crisp green salad.

Put the flour in a mixing bowl and make a well in the centre. Whisk the eggs, milk and water together and pour into the well. Stir carefully with a wooden spoon until you have a smooth batter. Let rest for 30 minutes.

Preheat the oven to 220°C (425°F) Gas 7. Grease a large roasting tin or 4–6 individual dishes and place in the oven.

Wrap the bacon around the sausages and place in the hot roasting tin or dishes. Add the onion, then pour in the batter. Return to the oven and bake for 30 minutes without opening the door. The batter should be light and well risen.

three-cheese cauliflower

Preparation 15 minutes

Cooking 30 minutes

Serves 4

1 cauliflower

100 g Gruyère cheese, grated

100 g Emmental cheese, grated

100 g Beaufort or other hard, strong cheese, grated

1 teaspoon cornflour

sea salt and freshly ground black pepper

a shallow, 20 x 26 cm ovenproof dish

How can you improve on classic comfort food? In this case, use a variety of cheeses to make it even richer.

Preheat the oven to 190°C (375°F) Gas 5.

Cut the cauliflower into florets and plunge them into boiling water. Bring back to the boil, then simmer for 4 minutes and drain well.

Put the cheeses in a bowl, sprinkle in the cornflour and mix to coat the cheese evenly. Transfer to a non-stick saucepan, add 200 ml water and gently bring to a slight simmer, stirring constantly until you have a smooth sauce.

Place the cauliflower in the ovenproof dish and pour the cheese sauce all over it. Bake in the oven for 15 minutes, until golden on top. Take care when serving as the cheese gets extremely hot.

lancashire hotpot

Preparation 15 minutes
Cooking 2 hours 15 minutes
Serves 4–6

2 tablespoons olive oil
800 g lamb neck fillet, cut into 5-cm pieces
1 onion, finely diced
2 carrots, finely diced
4 celery sticks, finely diced
2 leeks, thinly sliced
2 tablespoons plain flour
1 tablespoon Worcestershire sauce
800 g potatoes, unpeeled
sea salt and freshly ground black pepper

Inspired by thrift, this dish has transcended its humble origins and become a firm favourite around the world. The golden potato topping hides tender lamb in heavenly gravy.

Heat the olive oil in a large, flameproof casserole dish, add the lamb and brown all over. Transfer to a plate. Reduce the heat under the casserole, add all the vegetables then sauté for 10 minutes, stirring frequently.

Remove the casserole from the heat, add the meat, then sprinkle in the flour and mix well. Pour in just enough hot water to cover the meat and vegetables, stir well and return to the heat.

Preheat the oven to 180°C (350°F) Gas 4.

Bring the casserole to the boil, stirring frequently as the gravy thickens. Season and add the Worcestershire sauce. Remove from the heat.

Slice the potatoes thinly by hand or with a mandolin. Layer them carefully over the meat and vegetables, covering them completely. Place in the oven and cook for 2 hours. The potatoes should be golden on top and the gravy bubbling up around the sides.

easy tuna fish cakes

Preparation 15 minutes
Cooking 40 minutes
Serves 4

600 g sweet potatoes, peeled
and chopped
300 g tuna, flaked
2 spring onions, chopped
1 egg
100 g polenta
3 tablespoons olive oil
sea salt and freshly ground black pepper
1 lemon, to serve

Polenta is cornmeal, and it makes a lovely crumb coating on these fish cakes. If using canned tuna, buy a good-quality brand that has a dense texture and large chunks. Alternatively, pan-cook fresh tuna and flake it yourself.

Cook the sweet potatoes in a pan of simmering water for 20 minutes. Drain well and mash. Add the tuna, spring onions and egg, season and mix well. Divide the mixture into 8 equal pieces and shape into patties.

Put the polenta on a plate and dip the fish cakes in it until coated on all sides.

Heat the oil and fry the fish cakes on each side until golden. Serve with lemon wedges and a tomato salad.

parma ham-wrapped salmon on mash

Preparation 15 minutes
Cooking 25 minutes
Serves 4

800 g potatoes, unpeeled and diced
1 egg
50 g butter
4 salmon fillets, about 125 g each,
skinned and boned
4 slices Parma ham
a bunch of dill, chopped
sea salt and freshly ground black pepper

Fish such as salmon are rich in omega oils, which are essential for a healthy heart, so here's a recipe that will do your family some extra good!

Preheat the oven to 180°C (350°F) Gas 4, then lightly oil a baking sheet.

Bring the potatoes to the boil in a pan of water, then simmer for 20 minutes, until soft. Drain and return to the pan, place over the heat and shake to remove any excess moisture. Mash well, then mix in the egg and seasoning. Add the butter and mash again until creamy.

Meanwhile, season the salmon fillets and wrap in the Parma ham. Place on the prepared baking sheet and cook in the oven for 15 minutes. Sprinkle with the dill and serve with the mashed potatoes.

field mushroom tortilla

Preparation 15 minutes
Cooking 20 minutes
Serves 4–6

20 g butter
2 tablespoons olive oil
3 cooked potatoes, diced
200 g flat field mushrooms
1 garlic clove, crushed
125 g young spinach
4 eggs
100 ml milk
sea salt and freshly ground black pepper

Mushrooms can be an acquired taste among younger members of the family, but this will tempt them to try.

Heat the butter and olive oil in metal-handled frying pan, add the potatoes and brown on all sides. Transfer to a plate, then cook the mushrooms on both sides for 5 minutes, adding a little more oil or butter if necesary. Transfer to another plate and return the potatoes to the pan. Sprinkle in the garlic, then add the mushrooms and spinach.

Mix the eggs and milk together, season and pour into the pan. Cover and cook gently for 5 minutes.

Heat the grill to medium-high, place the tortilla under it and grill for 6–8 minutes, or until golden on top. Check that the egg is set, then serve hot or cold.

green bean risotto

Preparation 15 minutes
Cooking 30 minutes
Serves 4

1 litre chicken or vegetable stock
1 tablespoon olive oil
1 onion, finely chopped
1 garlic clove, crushed
300 g arborio rice
100 g runner beans, cut into 2-cm pieces
100 g peas, fresh or frozen
(no need to thaw)
100 g asparagus, cut into 2-cm pieces
100 g spinach, chopped
125 g Parmesan cheese, grated
sea salt and freshly ground black pepper

'Lip-smacking' is how my children describe this creamy risotto. The vegetables can be varied according to what you like and what's in season.

Put the stock in a saucepan and bring to a simmer.

Heat the olive oil in a shallow saucepan and sauté the onions and garlic on a low heat for 5 minutes without browning. Add the rice and stir well to coat in the oil. Add a ladleful of hot stock, stir and simmer until absorbed. Repeat until almost all the stock has been added.

Add all the vegetables with the last ladleful of stock, mix well and cook for 2 minutes. The rice should be *al dente*. Stir in half the Parmesan and add some seasoning. When ready to serve, offer the remaining Parmesan separately, plus a little extra olive oil for drizzling if you wish.

get-ahead weekends

Weekends are precious, so if you can get some of the meals planned and prepared in advance, it will give you more time to get out and about with the family, play sports, see friends, ferry the kids to parties or just enjoy life at home. This section offers lots of ideas to help you do just this.

When cooking during the week, I often try to get ahead by making something for the weekend too. Soups, for example, can be refrigerated or frozen and make a good lunch with fresh bread, a chunk of cheese and some fruit. Casseroles, curries and bakes are also good, as they reheat well, and marinated meats can be griddled or barbecued in a matter of minutes.

On wet weekends my children are often very happy to test their skills in the kitchen, especially if pizzas are on the menu. We all add our own favourite toppings, and what might otherwise be a chore becomes fun. Why not try this with your family?

golden butternut squash soup

Preparation 20 minutes
Cooking 40 minutes
Serves 4

1 kg butternut squash, peeled
2 tablespoons olive oil
2 onions, diced
1 garlic clove, crushed
1.2 litres chicken or vegetable stock
sea salt and freshly ground black pepper
single cream, to serve (optional)

Squash is a wonderfully versatile vegetable, and it's used to great effect in this flavoursome soup.

Cut the squash in half lengthways and use a spoon to scoop out the seeds. Chop the squash into 2-cm pieces.

Heat the oil in a large saucepan, add the squash, onions and garlic and sauté on a low heat for 10 minutes. Add the stock, bring to the boil, then simmer for 30 minutes.

Using a hand-held blender, blitz the soup until smooth and creamy. Season and serve with a drizzle of cream, if liked.

sausage and bean soup

Preparation 15 minutes
Cooking 35 minutes
Serves 4

2 tablespoons olive oil
1 onion, diced
2 garlic cloves, crushed
2 carrots, diced
2 celery sticks, diced
1.2 litres vegetable, ham or chicken stock
150 g cooked butter beans
1 bay leaf
a sprig of thyme
350 g Toulouse sausage
a handful of fresh parsley, chopped
sea salt and freshly ground black pepper

Toulouse sausage, made from pork, is the key ingredient in this recipe. Its coarse texture lends itself to this tasty, peasant-style soup.

Heat the oil in a saucepan, add the onion, garlic, carrots and celery and sauté on a low heat for 10 minutes, until soft. Add the stock, beans, bay leaf, thyme and sausages, season and simmer for 25 minutes.

Discard the bay leaf and thyme, then remove the sausages from the pan and slice them. Return to the pan, add the parsley and stir well.

onion soup

Preparation 20 minutes
Cooking 1 hour 15 minutes
Serves 4

1 tablespoon olive oil
25 g butter
600 g onions, thinly sliced
2 garlic cloves, crushed
2 tablespoons plain flour
1 litre beef or vegetable stock
200 ml red wine
1 bay leaf and a sprig of thyme
a bunch of parsley, finely chopped
4 slices French bread
100 g Gruyère cheese, grated
sea salt and freshly ground black pepper

A traditional French soup that never fails to please. It's always a meal in itself.

Heat the oil and butter in a medium pan, add the onions and garlic and sauté over a low heat for 25 minutes, stirring frequently. The onions should become golden brown and soft.

Sprinkle in the flour and stir to absorb the excess oil. Slowly pour in the stock and wine, mix well and bring to a gentle simmer. Add the bay leaf, thyme and seasoning. Cover and simmer for 40 minutes on a low heat.

Just before serving, toast the bread under the grill, top with the grated cheese and grill until melted. Stir the parsley into the soup, ladle it into bowls and top with the cheesy toasts.

minestrone with pesto

Preparation 15 minutes
+ overnight soaking
Cooking 2 hours 15 minutes
Serves 4

150 g dried haricot beans
1 tablespoon olive oil
1 red onion, chopped
2 garlic cloves, crushed
2 leeks, 2 carrots and 2 celery sticks, diced
1.2 litres chicken or vegetable stock
180 g lardons, diced
1½ tablespoons tomato purée
1 bay leaf and a small bunch of thyme
75 g tiny pasta
Pesto
75 g pine nuts
a generous bunch of basil
75 g Parmesan cheese, grated
2 garlic cloves, crushed
100 ml olive oil

Everyone loves classic minestrone, but for a change you could add some cooked ham or dried chillies. You could also use canned haricot beans instead of dried.

Cover the haricot beans in cold water and soak overnight. Drain, cover with fresh water and bring to the boil. Bubble hard for 10 minutes, then simmer for 1½ hours. Drain and set aside.

Heat the oil in a saucepan, add the onion, garlic, leeks, carrots, celery and lardons and sauté for 10 minutes over a medium heat without browning. Add the beans, stock, tomato purée and herbs, bring to the boil and simmer for 25 minutes.

Meanwhile, make the pesto. Put all the ingredients in a blender or food processor and whiz until smooth. Transfer to a jar, cover with olive oil and store in the fridge until needed.

When the soup has finished its first simmering, add the pasta and simmer again for 8 minutes, stirring frequently. Season and serve with a spoonful of pesto and lots of crusty bread.

mince and mash pie

Preparation 25 minutes
Cooking 1 hour 15 minutes
Serves 6

1 tablespoon olive oil
1 onion, diced
2 garlic cloves, crushed
1 celery stick, diced
1 carrot, diced
700 g minced lamb
25 g plain flour
300 ml stock
1 tablespoon Worcestershire sauce
900 g potatoes
25 g butter
50 ml milk
1 egg
sea salt and freshly ground black pepper
grated cheese, for sprinkling (optional)

You can use beef instead of lamb in this pie, or even half and half. Grated cheese makes a lovely topping.

Preheat the oven to 180°C (350°F) Gas 4.

Heat the oil in a large casserole, add the onion, garlic, celery and carrot and sauté over a low heat for 10 minutes. Add the lamb and cook for 5 minutes, breaking up the meat with a wooden spoon. Sprinkle in the flour, mix well, then add the stock, Worcestershire sauce and seasoning. Stir well, then cover and set aside.

Cook the potatoes in a pan of boiling water for 20 minutes, drain well, return to the pan and shake over a low heat to steam off any excess moisture. Remove from the heat and mash until smooth. Add the butter, milk, egg and seasoning and beat well. Spoon the potato over the lamb in the casserole and use a fork to spread it evenly. Sprinkle with grated cheese, if liked. Bake in the oven for 40 minutes.

macaroni, spinach and cheese bake

Preparation 10 minutes
Cooking 40 minutes
Serves 4

250 g macaroni
50 g butter
50 g plain flour
500 ml milk
150 g cooked spinach, well drained
200 g Parmesan cheese, grated
sea salt and freshly ground black pepper

a large ovenproof baking dish

Fresh or frozen spinach can be used in this recipe, but do make sure that both are thoroughly drained.

Cook the macaroni according to the packet instructions. Preheat the oven to 190°C (375°F) Gas 5.

Meanwhile, melt the butter in a saucepan, remove from the heat and mix in the flour to make a roux. Return to a low heat and slowly pour in the milk, stirring constantly. Bring to the boil and cook for 1 minute, stirring frequently.

Drain the macaroni and add to the sauce along with the spinach, seasoning and half the cheese. Mix well. Pour the mixture into the ovenproof baking dish, scatter the remaining cheese on top and bake for 15 minutes, until golden.

beef and carrot casserole with cheesy dumplings

Preparation 30 minutes
Cooking 2 hours
Serves 4–6

1 tablespoon olive oil
2 garlic cloves, crushed
1 onion, diced
2 celery sticks, diced
800 g chuck steak, cut into cubes
400 ml beef stock
200 ml red wine
2 bay leaves
4 carrots, cut into small chunks
25 g plain flour
sea salt and freshly ground black pepper

Dumplings
200 g plain flour
75 g hard vegetable fat
1 teaspoon baking powder
75 g strong Cheddar cheese, grated

Think of chilly, dark evenings and this is exactly what you'd want to eat. The feather-light dumplings nestling in the rich, savoury casserole will have everyone demanding more.

Heat the oil in a large casserole, add the garlic, onion and celery and sauté for 4 minutes. Transfer to a plate. Put the beef in the casserole, increase the heat and sauté for 6 minutes, stirring frequently. When the beef is cooked, return the onion mixture to the casserole. Add the stock, red wine, seasoning and bay leaves, bring to the boil, then reduce the heat to a gentle simmer. Cover and cook for 1¹/₂ hours.

To make the dumplings, place the flour and baking powder in a bowl and rub in the fat until it resembles breadcrumbs. Add the cheese, mixing it in with a knife. Add 75–100 ml water and use your hands to bring the mixture together and form a dough. Divide into 8 equal pieces and roll into balls.

Remove the casserole from the heat for 5 minutes, then sift in the flour and stir to thicken the gravy. Return to the heat, add the carrots and stir until the casserole comes to a simmer. Place the dumplings on top, cover and cook for 20 minutes.

spaghetti bolognese

Preparation 20 minutes
Cooking 1 hour 15 minutes
Serves 4–6

2 tablespoons olive oil
3 garlic cloves, crushed
2 onions, diced
1 celery stick, diced
1 carrot, diced
700 g minced beef
a bunch of oregano, chopped
a sprig of thyme
2 bay leaves
2 tablespoons tomato purée
1 litre tomato passata
300 g spaghetti
a handful of parsley, chopped
sea salt and freshly ground black pepper
freshly grated Parmesan cheese, to serve

Long, slow cooking is the secret of good bolognese sauce. It can be served with any shape of pasta, and a crisp green salad is the perfect accompaniment.

Heat the oil in a large saucepan, add the garlic, onions, celery and carrot and sauté gently for 10 minutes. Add the beef, breaking it up with a wooden spoon, and cook for a further 10 minutes. Add the oregano, thyme, bay leaves, tomato purée and passata, season and mix well. Simmer for 1 hour, stirring frequently.

Cook the spaghetti according to the packet instructions. Drain well and divide between individual plates. Stir the parsley into the sauce, then spoon onto the pasta and serve.

chilli con carne

Preparation 20 minutes
Cooking 1 hour 15 minutes
Serves 4–6

1 quantity bolognese sauce (see above)
1 tablespoon cayenne pepper
1 tablespoon paprika
1 glass of red wine
2 x 400-g cans red kidney beans, drained and rinsed
a handful of coriander, chopped

Simple dishes are often the best, and they don't come much simpler than this. You can add more or less cayenne pepper, depending on how hot you like your food.

Make the bolognese sauce as described above, but also add the cayenne, paprika, wine and beans listed here before simmering for 1 hour.

Just before serving, stir in the coriander and serve with bread or boiled rice and a bowl of guacamole (see page 39).

traditional fish cakes

Preparation 40 minutes
Cooking 40 minutes
Serves 4

800 g potatoes, peeled
50 g butter
50 ml milk
400 g salmon, cod or halibut, skinned
3 eggs
a bunch of parsley, chopped
100 g plain flour, plus extra for dusting
200 g breadcrumbs
300 ml olive oil
sea salt and freshly ground black pepper

These fish cakes freeze well, so are useful for get-ahead weekends. Any type of fish can be used.

Cook the potatoes in boiling water for 20 minutes, Drain, return to the pan and shake over a low heat to dry off. Mash the potatoes, add the butter and milk and mix well.

Preheat the oven to 180°C (350°F) Gas 4. Lightly oil a shallow ovenproof dish. Put the fish into the prepared dish, cover with foil and bake for 10 minutes. Set aside to cool, then flake the fish into the potato. Beat one egg and add to the mixture, followed by the parsley and seasoning. Mix well.

Put the flour, breadcrumbs and remaining eggs in 3 separate bowls. Whisk the eggs. Divide the fish mixture into 8 equal pieces and shape into patties. Dust each fish cake with flour, then use one hand to dip them into the egg; use the other hand to coat in the breadcrumbs. Try to get an even coating.

Heat the oil and fry the fish cakes on each side for 5 minutes, until golden. Serve with hollandaise sauce (see page 116).

vegetable, seed and nut cakes

Preparation 40 minutes
Cooking 40 minutes
Serves 4

500 g mashed potato
200 g cooked spinach
300 ml olive oil
100 g mushrooms, chopped
1 garlic clove, crushed
1 courgette, grated
100 g pumpkin seeds
40 g sesame seeds
100 g peanuts, chopped
sea salt and freshly ground black pepper

A delicious alternative to fish cakes, especially if you have vegetarians in the family, but even non-veggies will happily tuck into these.

Mix the mashed potato with the spinach in a bowl. Heat 1 tablespoon of the oil in a frying pan, gently sauté the mushrooms and garlic for 5 minutes, then add to the potato mixture. Add the courgette and seasoning and stir well. Divide into 8 equal pieces and roll into balls.

Mix the seeds and nuts together on a large plate and roll the balls in the mixture to coat well. Gently flatten them into patties. Heat the remaining oil in a frying pan and cook the patties on each side until golden, about 3–4 minutes.

thai green chicken curry

Preparation 20 minutes
Cooking 20 minutes
Serves 4

2 tablespoons vegetable oil
1 onion, sliced
5 cm fresh ginger, peeled and sliced
2 garlic cloves, crushed
1 lemongrass stick, chopped
1 mild green chilli, diced
4 chicken fillets, sliced
2 kaffir lime leaves
2 tablespoons Thai green curry paste
200 ml coconut milk
juice of 1 lime
75 g broccoli florets
75 g green beans, trimmed
sea salt and freshly ground black pepper
a bunch of basil, to serve

There is a wonderful fragrance to Thai curries, and they make a fantastic family meal. Build up the chilli content gradually until you find a spiciness that everyone enjoys.

Heat the oil in a large saucepan, add the onion, ginger, garlic, lemongrass and chilli and cook over a low heat for 5 minutes. Add the chicken and cook for a further 5 minutes.

Add the kaffir lime leaves and curry paste and mix well. Shake the can of coconut milk and slowly pour into the curry, mixing constantly. Pour in 100 ml water and the lime juice, bring to a simmer and cook gently for 5 minutes. Add the broccoli and beans and simmer for another 3 minutes. Serve in bowls, topped with torn basil leaves. Plain boiled jasmine rice is a good accompaniment.

indian lamb curry

Preparation 20 minutes
Cooking 1 hour 30 minutes–2 hours
Serves 4–6

2 tablespoons vegetable oil
1 onion, sliced
5 cm fresh ginger, peeled and chopped
1 mild red chilli, chopped
3 garlic cloves, crushed
1 teaspoon garam masala
1 teaspoon mild curry powder
800 g lamb neck fillet, cut into 3-cm pieces
1 x 400-g can chopped tomatoes
a bunch of coriander, chopped
sea salt and freshly ground black pepper

Get the younger family members to help with all the chopping in this recipe. My boys love the different colours and smells.

Heat half the oil in a large pan, add the onion, ginger, chilli and garlic and cook on a high heat for 1 minute, stirring constantly. Add the spices and cook for a further minute. Transfer to a plate.

Heat the remaining tablespoon of oil in the pan and fry the lamb briskly until browned, about 5 minutes. Return the onion mixture to the pan and add the tomatoes. Season and pour in just enough water to cover. Bring to the boil, then lower the heat, cover and simmer for 1½–2 hours, stirring occasionally. The lamb should be tender and the sauce thick.

Just before serving, add the coriander. Serve with basmati rice and a bowl of natural yoghurt to calm down the spiciness.

prawn curry

Preparation 15 minutes
Cooking 15 minutes
Serves 4

2 tablespoons vegetable oil
1 onion, grated
3 garlic cloves, crushed
5 cm fresh ginger, peeled and sliced
1 mild red chilli, chopped
1 teaspoon turmeric
2 teaspoons curry powder
1 teaspoon ground coriander
1 teaspoon ground cumin
400 g cooked peeled prawns, defrosted
1 x 400-g can chopped tomatoes
juice of 2 limes
a bunch of chopped coriander
sea salt and freshly ground black pepper

Tiger prawns or large peeled prawns are ideal for this colourful, citrus-flavoured curry.

Heat the oil in a large pan, add the onion, garlic, ginger and chilli and cook for 5 minutes over a medium heat. Add the turmeric, curry powder, ground coriander and cumin and mix well. Add the prawns and cook for 3 minutes.

Pour in the tomatoes and lime juice, season and bring to the boil. Reduce the heat and simmer for 5 minutes. Add the chopped coriander and serve with basmati rice.

vegetable curry

Preparation 30 minutes
Cooking 30 minutes
Serves 4–8

2 tablespoons vegetable oil
1 red onion, sliced
1 garlic clove, crushed
2 mild chillies (1 red, 1 green), chopped
1 teaspoon curry powder
1 teaspoon ground coriander
1/2 teaspoon fenugreek
300 g potatoes, chopped
300 g butternut squash, chopped
1 aubergine, chopped
1 courgette, chopped
150 g green beans, trimmed
200 g natural bio yoghurt
a bunch of coriander, chopped
sea salt and freshly ground black pepper

Indian cuisine has a huge variety of vegetable curries, and this recipe offers one that is simple yet very satisfying – perfect weekend fare.

Heat the oil in a large frying pan, add the onion, garlic and chillies and sauté for 5 minutes. Stir in the curry powder, coriander and fenugreek. Add the potatoes, squash, aubergine and courgette and mix well to cover in the spices. Pour in 300 ml water, then cover and simmer for 20 minutes, stirring occasionally. Add more water if needed.

When the vegetables are tender, add the green beans, then season and cook for 5 minutes. Remove from the heat, let cool for 3 minutes, then add the yoghurt and coriander. Mix well and serve with warm naan bread.

lamb pilaf

Preparation 15 minutes
Cooking 2 hours
Serves 4

3 tablespoons olive oil
1 onion, chopped
2 garlic cloves, crushed
5 cardamom pods, crushed
1 cinnamon stick
3 bay leaves
50 g almonds
500 g lamb neck fillet, cut into 3-cm pieces
50 g sultanas
50 g dried apricots
300 g basmati rice
a handful of chopped parsley (optional)

Pilafs are rice dishes that originated in the Middle East. They can be made with meat, poultry or seafood, and spiced in a variety of ways.

Heat 1 tablespoon of the oil in a large casserole dish, add the onion and garlic and fry for 5 minutes. Add the cardamom, cinnamon, bay leaves and almonds and cook for a further 4 minutes. Transfer to a plate.

Heat the remaining oil and fry the lamb on a high heat until browned all over. Return the onion mixture to the pan along with the sultanas and apricots. Pour in just enough water to cover, then bring to the boil, cover and simmer for $1\frac{1}{2}$ hours.

Add the rice, stir well and cover with water. Bring to the boil, then cover and simmer very gently for 30 minutes. Add the chopped parsley, if liked, and serve.

spare ribs

Preparation 10 minutes
+ overnight marinating
Cooking 50 minutes
Serves 4

16 pork spare ribs
Marinade
1 tablespoon runny honey
1 tablespoon dark soy sauce
2 garlic cloves, crushed
zest and juice of 1 unwaxed lemon
1 tablespoon unrefined caster sugar
2 tablespoons tomato purée
1 tablespoon Worcestershire sauce
1 teaspoon red wine vinegar
2 teaspoons Dijon mustard
sea salt and freshly ground black pepper

Finger food comes in all shapes and sizes, but none better than these yummy spare ribs – a lovely weekend treat for all the family.

Put all the marinade ingredients in a large bowl and mix until smooth. Add the ribs to the bowl, turn to coat and let marinate overnight, turning frequently.

Preheat the oven to 180°C (350°F) Gas 4, then lightly oil a roasting tin.

Transfer the ribs to the prepared roasting tin, cover with foil and bake for 30 minutes. Remove the foil and bake for a further 10 minutes, basting now and again. Turn the ribs and cook for a further 10 minutes, continuing to baste occasionally. Serve with noodles, rice or salad.

tomato, basil and mozzarella pizza

Younger family members never seem to tire of pizza, so get them involved in the making as well as the eating.

Preparation 40 minutes + 1–2 hours proving
Cooking 40 minutes
Serves 2

450 g plain flour
14 g quick yeast
a pinch of salt
a pinch of sugar
225 ml warm water
2 tablespoons olive oil
Topping
4 tablespoons olive oil
1 small onion, finely diced
2 garlic cloves, crushed
300 ml tomato passata
a pinch of dried oregano
200 g cherry tomatoes
2 mozzarella balls, sliced
a large bunch of basil
sea salt and freshly ground black pepper

Put the flour, yeast, salt and sugar in a bowl, make a well in the centre, then add the water and oil and gradually draw in the flour to make a smooth dough. Knead for 12 minutes on a lightly floured work surface. Return the dough to the bowl, drizzle with a little oil, then cover and leave in a warm place until doubled in size. This will take 1–2 hours, depending on the temperature.

To make the topping, heat half the oil in a medium saucepan, add the onion and garlic and sauté on a medium heat for 6 minutes. Add the passata, oregano and the remaining oil, season and bring to a simmer. Cook for 25 minutes, stirring frequently. The sauce should be thick and full of flavour.

Preheat the oven to 190°C (375°F) Gas 5. Lightly oil 2 baking sheets. Knock the air out of the dough and knead for 5 minutes. Cut the dough in half, roll each piece into a ball and let rest for 10 minutes. Lightly flour a work surface and flatten each piece of dough into a circle about 25 cm in diameter. Place each on a prepared baking sheet and add the tomato mixture, spreading it with the back of a spoon. Top with the cherry tomatoes and sliced mozzarella, season and drizzle with a little extra olive oil. Put in the oven and bake for 12–15 minutes. Scatter with torn basil leaves, then cut into wedges and serve.

sunday lunch

There's no doubt that Sunday lunch is the highlight of the week in many families – even in these days of fast food. Everyone loves the succulent roast with all the trimmings, and every family has its own special recipes and traditions associated with it. Some have mint sauce with lamb, others prefer redcurrant jelly. (I serve both.) Some have Yorkshire pudding with roast beef; others have it with everything. Whatever your preferences, I think it's essential to make real gravy, using the juices from the roasting tin. Nothing out of a packet or jar tastes as good.

Of course, Sunday lunch does not have to be a roast: it can be anything you like – perhaps a homemade egg and bacon tart or a large dish of lasagne. Whatever you make, don't forget to serve vegetables. Choose the best of what's in season and prepare them a little differently to tempt everyone to have some. Spiced red cabbage, roast sesame carrots and cauliflower in cheese sauce are just a few of the possibilities. Make your Sunday lunch a tradition that no one will want to miss.

roast chicken with lemon, thyme and potato stuffing

Preparation 20 minutes
Cooking approx. 1 hour 20 minutes
Serves 4

1 medium free-range chicken
1 unwaxed lemon, thinly sliced
4 bay leaves
4 rashers of bacon
Stuffing
2 garlic cloves, crushed
1 onion, finely diced
leaves from 4 sprigs of thyme
1 large potato, coarsely grated
300 g sausagemeat
zest and juice of 1 unwaxed lemon
sea salt and freshly ground black pepper
Gravy
25 g plain flour
500 ml chicken stock
sea salt and freshly ground black pepper

For me, the smell of roasting chicken conjures up childhood memories of a cosy Sunday at home, so now I often cook it for my own family. It's always worth cooking a larger bird than you need because the leftovers can be used in a pilaf or to make sandwiches. You can also use the carcass to make stock and freeze it for making soup or risotto. Three meals for the price of one bird!

Preheat the oven to 180°C (350°F) Gas 4. Lightly oil a roasting tin.

Take the chicken and carefully slide your hand between the skin and the breast meat. Insert the lemon slices under the skin along with the bay leaves.

To make the stuffing, put the garlic, onion, thyme, potato and sausagemeat in a large bowl. Add the lemon zest and juice, season and mix well. Cut any excess fat from the cavity of the chicken, then stuff the bird with the potato mixture.

Weigh your chicken to work out the cooking time: you should allow 20 minutes per 500 g, plus 20 minutes extra. Put the chicken in the prepared roasting tin and lay the bacon rashers over the breast. Put in the hot oven and cook for the time you have calculated. When the chicken is ready, remove it from the roasting tin and keep warm.

Now make the gravy. Add the flour to the tin and stir with a wooden spoon to combine with the fat and juices. Slowly pour in the chicken stock, stirring continuously to prevent lumps forming. Place the roasting tin directly on the heat and bring to the boil. When the mixture has thickened, remove it from the heat and season well. If you like a very smooth gravy, press it through a sieve with the back of a spoon.

Carve the chicken and serve with the stuffing, a selection of trimmings (see page 100) and the hot gravy.

butterflied leg of lamb with mediterranean stuffing

Preparation 30 minutes
Cooking 1 hour 30 minutes
Serves 6

1.5-kg leg of lamb, butterflied
Stuffing
leaves from 2 sprigs of rosemary
2 red onions, finely chopped
3 garlic cloves, finely chopped
75 g olives, stoned and chopped
1 courgette, grated and squeezed dry
1 egg
1 tablespoon olive oil
sea salt and freshly ground black pepper
Gravy
2 tablespoons plain flour
1 teaspoon tomato purée
3 tablespoons redcurrant jelly
100 ml red wine
200 ml vegetable stock
sea salt and freshly ground black pepper

Your butcher will butterfly the joint for you, but if you want to do it yourself, hold a very sharp knife like a dagger and cut from the fleshy end of the leg to the opposite end. Then let your knife follow the bones, cutting the flesh away so that the meat opens out like a butterfly.

Preheat the oven to 190°C (375°F) Gas 5, then lightly oil a roasting tin.

Combine all the stuffing ingredients and season. Open out the leg of lamb, skin-side down, and spread the stuffing over it. Fold the lamb back together and tie securely with string. Place the lamb in the prepared tin and roast for 1 hour and 20 minutes. When cooked, transfer the lamb to a carving plate and keep warm.

Pour half the fat out of the roasting tin, add the flour and mix until smooth. Stir in the tomato purée and redcurrant jelly, then pour in the wine and stock, mixing thoroughly. Place the tin directly on the heat and stir constantly until the gravy thickens. Adjust the seasoning and press the gravy through a sieve to remove any lumps. Cut the string from the lamb and carve. Serve with mashed potatoes and green beans.

crunchy roast pork
with baked stuffed apples

Preparation 20 minutes

Cooking 1 hour 30 minutes

Serves 6

1.5-kg loin of pork, boned and rolled

3 eating apples

1 onion, chopped

8 sage leaves, chopped

1 tablespoon olive oil

sea salt and freshly ground black pepper

Gravy

2 tablespoons plain flour

200 ml white wine

200 ml vegetable stock

sea salt and freshly ground black pepper

Get your butcher to score lines in the skin about 2 cm apart: this will produce fantastic crackling, which many people regard as the highlight of roast pork.

Preheat the oven to 220°C (425°F) Gas 7, then lightly oil a roasting tin.

Dry the loin of pork with kitchen paper, place in the prepared tin and roast for 30 minutes. Reduce the heat to 180°C (350°F) Gas 4 and cook the pork for a further 30 minutes.

Slice the apples in half across the middle and cut out the core. Mix the onion and sage with the oil and season. Arrange the apple halves around the roasting pork and fill the cavities with the stuffing. Return to the oven and cook for 30 minutes. When cooked, transfer the pork and apples to a carving plate and keep warm.

To make the gravy, drain half the fat from the roasting tin, add the flour and mix until smooth. Pour in the wine and stock and mix thoroughly. Place the roasting tin directly over the heat and keep stirring until the gravy thickens. Adjust the seasoning. For a very smooth gravy, press it through a sieve. Serve the pork with the roast apples, a selection of vegetables (see page 100) and the gravy.

roast duck with citrus fruits

Preparation 15 minutes
Cooking 2 hours 30 minutes
Serves 4

1 x 3-kg duck
1 unwaxed lemon, thinly sliced
1 unwaxed orange, thinly sliced
1 unwaxed lime, thinly sliced
Orange sauce
1 tablespoon plain flour
150 ml vegetable stock
150 ml orange juice
sea salt and freshly ground black pepper

Duck has a wonderful flavour, but it is a fatty meat, so this recipe contains citrus fruit to help cut through the richness. Do not be alarmed at the size of the duck specified; it loses a huge amount of fat during cooking, and has much less meat than a chicken of the same size.

Preheat the oven to 190°C (375°F) Gas 5. Lightly grease a roasting tin.

Put all the slices of citrus fruit in the cavity of the duck. Rub seasoning all over the skin. Place the duck on a roasting rack in the prepared tin; this is important so that the fat can drip out and the duck will not be sitting in it. Place in the oven and roast for 2½ hours.

When cooked, lift up the duck and pour the juices from the cavity into a heatproof jug. Transfer the duck to a carving plate and keep warm while making the sauce.

To make the orange sauce, drain all but 1 tablespoon of fat from the roasting tin (save the excess in the fridge for general cooking purposes). Add the flour to the tin and mix thoroughly. Stir in the stock and orange juice, and add the reserved duck juices. Place over the heat and bring to the boil, stirring constantly. If you want a very smooth sauce, press the mixture through a sieve. Carve the duck and serve with carrots, roast potatoes and the orange sauce.

sunday lunch trimmings

Every good roast needs the traditional accompaniments to take it to the next level of deliciousness. All the ideas below serve 4.

roast potatoes

12–16 potatoes, peeled
4 tablespoons duck or goose fat or olive oil

Preheat the oven to 180°C (350°F) Gas 4. Parboil the potatoes for 12 minutes, then drain and shake in the colander to roughen up the outsides. Heat the fat in a large roasting tin in the oven and, when very hot, carefully add the potatoes, turning to coat them in the hot oil. Return to the oven and cook for 40 minutes. Do not disturb them before that or you will spoil their chances of crisping up. Turn them and cook for another 20 minutes.

roast sesame beetroot, parsnips and carrots

20 g butter
2 tablespoons olive oil
200 g each beetroot, parsnips and carrots, peeled and chopped
2 tablespoons sesame seeds

Preheat the oven to 180°C (350°F) Gas 4. Heat the butter and oil in a roasting tin, add the vegetables and toss to coat. Put in the oven and roast for 35 minutes. Remove and turn with a spoon to ensure even cooking. Sprinkle with the sesame seeds and return to the oven for a further 20 minutes.

cauliflower with cheese sauce

1 cauliflower, cut into florets
25 g butter
40 g plain flour
600 ml milk
175 g Cheddar or other hard cheese, grated

Preheat the oven to 180°C (350°F) Gas 4. Steam the cauliflower over a pan of boiling water for 5 minutes. Melt the butter in a small saucepan, stir in the flour to make a smooth paste, then add the milk. Stir constantly until it thickens, then add 150 g of the cheese, stirring until melted. Put the cauliflower in a buttered ovenproof dish and pour the sauce over it. Top with the remaining cheese and bake for 25 minutes.

steamed vegetables

Choose two or three vegetables for a Sunday lunch, allowing about 100–125g per person. Steam over a pan of boiling water for 3–4 minutes and serve lightly seasoned and tossed in a little olive oil or butter.

gravy variations

Follow the basic gravy method described on page 92, using the appropriate stock mixed half and half with wine or vegetable water if you wish.

Beef – add 1 teaspoon mild mustard.

Chicken – add the juice of 1 lemon.

Duck – substitute 100 ml stock with cranberry, orange or cherry juice.

Lamb – melt 100 g redcurrant jelly in the microwave and substitute for some of the liquid.

Pork – add 1 teaspoon mild mustard or a dash of soy sauce, or substitute 100 ml of the stock with the same quantity of apple juice or cider.

In the summer serve any of these roasts with green sauce (see page 118) for a Mediterranean-flavoured meal.

fish and prawn kedgeree

Preparation 20 minutes
Cooking 40 minutes
Serves 4

300 g brown basmati rice
375 g undyed smoked haddock
50 g butter
1 tablespoon oil
2 shallots, diced
200 g cooked peeled prawns
a handful of parsley, finely chopped
4 hard-boiled eggs, quartered
4 lemon wedges
sea salt and freshly ground black pepper

Originally an Indian dish, kedgeree was appropriated by the British during the days of the empire. It makes a good brunch dish.

Wash and cook the rice according to the packet instructions, then drain and place in a large bowl.

Preheat the oven to 180°C (350°F) Gas 4. Put the fish on a piece of foil, wrap loosely and place on a baking sheet in the oven for 10 minutes. When cooked and cool enough to handle, flake the fish onto the cooked rice.

Heat the butter and oil in a frying pan, add the shallots and sauté for 3 minutes. Add the prawns and sauté for a further 2 minutes. Mix into the rice, then season and add all but 1 tablespoon of the parsley. Transfer to a serving bowl.

Arrange the eggs on top of the rice, add the lemon wedges and scatter with the remaining parsley.

chicken in a pot

Preparation 20 minutes
Cooking 1 hour 15 minutes
Serves 4–6

1 medium free-range chicken
2 celery sticks, chopped
1 red onion, chopped
2 garlic cloves, finely sliced
3 carrots, chopped
1 turnip, about 200 g, chopped
2 bay leaves
1 sprig of rosemary
2 sprigs of thyme
8 small waxy potatoes
½ head of Savoy cabbage
sea salt and freshly ground black pepper

King Henry IV said that every family in France should be given the ingredients to make this dish once a week. Sound advice, as it's good-value family fare.

Cut any excess fat or skin off the chicken and place the bird in a large casserole. Add the celery, onion, garlic, carrots, turnip, herbs and seasoning. Add just enough water to cover, then place on the heat and bring to the boil. Reduce to a simmer, then cover and cook for 45 minutes. Add the potatoes and cook for a further 25 minutes. Spoon off any excess fat floating on the top of the casserole. Trim the cabbage and cut into 4 wedges, add to the pot, cover and cook for 4 minutes.

Remove the chicken, cut into joints and serve, ladling over the vegetables and stock at the table.

family and friends

Eating together with family and friends is one of life's great pleasures. Good food and conversation seem to go hand in hand, so it's great to cook up some favourite dishes and have a variety of generations sitting around the table and enjoying a fine meal that everyone has contributed to preparing.

To make life easier, the recipes in this section include several one-pot dishes, such as cassoulet and baked ham with layered potatoes, and perennial family favourites, such as meat loaf and burgers. When you're surrounded by loved ones, the food doesn't have to be grand – it just needs to be flavoursome, nutritious and abundant. The following recipes are just that.

chicken and bacon pot

Preparation 10 minutes
Cooking 45 minutes
Serves 4

1 tablespoon olive oil
300 g lardons
250 g button mushrooms
4 chicken breasts
1 garlic clove, crushed
2 shallots, diced
50 g plain flour
500 ml chicken stock
200 ml white wine
1 bay leaf
a handful of parsley, chopped
sea salt and freshly ground black pepper

The lardons add a special intensity to the flavour of this easy-to-make dish. Serve with rice to mop up the lovely sauce.

Heat the olive oil in a casserole dish, add the lardons and mushrooms and cook over a medium heat until golden. Transfer to a plate.

Put the chicken breasts in the casserole and quickly brown on both sides. Set aside with the lardons. Preheat the oven to 180°C (350°F) Gas 4.

Sauté the garlic and shallots over a low heat in the same pan for 5 minutes. Add the flour and mix well. Remove the pan from the heat, slowly pour in the stock and wine, and stir until smooth. Return to the heat and bring to the boil, stirring constantly. Mix in the lardons and mushrooms, then add the chicken breasts, bay leaf and seasoning. Cover and cook in the oven for 30 minutes. Add the parsley just before serving.

mediterranean garlic prawns

Preparation 40 minutes
Cooking 5 minutes
Serves 4

1.7 kg uncooked prawns, shells on, or 1 kg uncooked prawns, shelled and deveined
3 tablespoons olive oil
50 g butter
3 garlic cloves, crushed
a bunch of parsley, chopped
juice of 1 lemon
sea salt and freshly ground black pepper

Fantastically quick and easy to prepare, and a great favourite at family gatherings. Serve with a mixed salad and lots of crusty bread.

If using unshelled prawns, run a small, sharp knife down the back of each one and remove the black vein. Put the prawns in a colander, rinse well and drain thoroughly.

Heat the oil and butter in a large pan, add the garlic and prawns and cook for 3 minutes on a high heat, tossing well. The prawns are cooked through when they are totally pink all over. Add the parsley, lemon juice and seasoning, toss well and serve with plenty of warm bread for mopping up the yummy juices.

baked ham with
layered potatoes

Preparation 30 minutes + 1 hour soaking

Cooking 1 hour 20 minutes

Serves 6

1-kg ham joint, boned
900 g potatoes, peeled and thinly sliced
1–2 onions, thinly sliced
250 ml hot chicken or ham stock
25 g butter, melted
sea salt and freshly ground black pepper

a shallow ovenproof dish, 20 cm in diameter, buttered

Family meals don't come much simpler than this. For easier carving, ask your butcher to bone the ham joint for you.

Preheat the oven to 200°C (400°F) Gas 6.

If the ham joint is salty, cover it in cold water and leave to soak for 1 hour. Drain and pat dry with kitchen paper. Wrap the ham loosely in foil and put in a roasting tin. Bake for 1 hour 20 minutes (40 minutes per 500 g).

Meanwhile, put a layer of potatoes (overlapping slightly) in the prepared dish, top with a layer of onions and season with salt and pepper. Continue making layers, finishing with a layer of the potatoes. Push the layers down firmly with the palms of your hands. Pour the hot stock into the dish, brush the top with melted butter and cover with foil.

Bake the potatoes at the top of the oven with the ham for 50 minutes, then remove the foil and continue to cook for a further 30 minutes. The top should be golden brown and crunchy and the potatoes soft when a knife is inserted.

meat loaf with two sauces

Preparation 30 minutes
Cooking 1 hour 15 minutes
Serves 6

12 slices Parma ham
200 g chicken livers, chopped
400 g lean pork, diced
300 g minced turkey or chicken
1 red onion, diced
2 eggs, beaten
3 bay leaves, torn
a bunch of flat leaf parsley, chopped
sea salt and freshly ground black pepper
Tomato sauce and spiced tomato sauce
3 tablespoons olive oil
1 onion, diced
2 garlic cloves, crushed
2 x 400-g cans chopped tomatoes
1 red chilli, chopped

a 1-kg loaf tin

In France the humble meat loaf is called a 'terrine', which makes it sound a lot grander. Here it's served with two tomato sauces, one of which is spiced up for more adventurous eaters.

Preheat the oven to 170°C (325°F) Gas 3.

Line the loaf tin with the Parma ham, leaving some aside to cover the top of the finished meat loaf.

Put the chicken livers in a bowl with the pork and turkey, add the onion, eggs, bay leaves and parsley, season and mix well. This is best done with your hands.

Fill the prepared tin with the meat, flatten out the top and cover with the remaining ham. Cover with foil and bake in the oven for 1 hour 15 minutes. Remove and let stand for 10 minutes. Drain off any juice into a jug, then turn out the meat loaf onto a deep plate.

To make the tomato sauce, heat the oil and sauté the onion gently for 5 minutes. Add the garlic and cook for a further 5 minutes. Add the tomatoes and reserved meat juices, season and simmer gently for 30 minutes, stirring frequently.

To make the spiced tomato sauce, pour half of the tomato sauce mixture into another pan, add the chopped chilli and simmer for 10 minutes. Serve both sauces with the meat loaf.

homemade burgers

Preparation 30 minutes
Cooking 10 minutes
Makes 4

600 g lean minced beef
1 garlic clove, crushed
1 shallot, finely diced
a bunch of parsley, chopped
1 teaspoon Worcestershire sauce
4 slices streaky bacon
4 ciabatta rolls
4 tablespoons mayonnaise
4 slices beef tomato
100 g Cheddar cheese, grated (optional)
1 avocado, sliced
4 leaves iceberg lettuce, shredded
sea salt and freshly ground black pepper
olive oil, for frying

Burgers are fantastically versatile, so build yours just as you wish, with or without the suggested garnishes.

Put the mince, garlic, shallot, parsley and Worcestershire sauce in a large bowl, season and mix well with your hands. Divide the mixture into four and shape into burgers.

Heat some oil in a large frying pan and cook for 2 minutes on each side for rare, 3 minutes for medium-rare and 4 minutes for well done.

Meanwhile, grill the bacon until crisp. Cut the ciabatta rolls in half and grill the insides. Spread the grilled sides with mayonnaise. Put a slice of tomato on the grilled base and a burger on top, followed by a handful of cheese, if using, a bacon rasher, a slice or two of avocado and some lettuce. Sandwich together with the remaining bread and serve with ketchup and mustard.

cassoulet

Preparation 30 minutes
+ overnight soaking
Cooking 3 hours 30 minutes
Serves 4–6

300 g dried haricot beans
1 onion
1 carrot
4 tomatoes
1 bay leaf
1 sprig of thyme
a bunch of parsley
1 celery stick
400 g duck confit
4 Toulouse sausages
200 g belly pork, chopped
300 g lamb neck fillet, cubed
2 garlic cloves, slightly crushed
200 g breadcrumbs
sea salt and freshly ground black pepper

Although this famous French dish takes a while to make, it is well worth the effort. Any leftovers reheat well, so why not make a double quantity?

Soak the haricot beans overnight in a bowl of water. Drain and place in a saucepan, cover with fresh water and add the onion, carrot and tomatoes. Bring to the boil.

Meanwhile, tie the bay leaf, thyme, parsley and celery together with string (this makes removal easier) and add to the beans. Stir well and cook for 1½ hours, until the beans are soft. Add more water if needed while cooking, always keeping 2 cm of liquid above the beans.

Heat a little of the fat from the duck confit and brown the sausages in it. Set aside on a plate. Put the pork and lamb in the pan and cook over a high heat to seal the outside. When the beans are cooked, drain any excess liquid into the meat and simmer for 30 minutes.

Meanwhile, preheat the oven to 180ºC (350ºF) Gas 4. Rub the inside of a large casserole dish with the garlic and leave both cloves in the dish.

Discard the vegetables and herbs from the beans. Put a layer of beans in the prepared casserole dish, arrange all the meat, including the duck confit, on top, and cover with the remaining beans. Pour in as much cooking liquid as the dish will hold, then sprinkle with a layer of breadcrumbs. Place in the oven and cook for 1½ hours, stirring every 20 minutes and topping with a fresh layer of breadcrumbs (these help to thicken the cooking liquid).

When ready, the final breadcrumb topping should be golden, with the juices bubbling up around the edges. Serve with a simple green salad.

sauces

Extra flavour and complexity can be added to savoury dishes by serving them with an additional sauce. Here are some ideas.

mustard mayo

Great with new potatoes and burgers, and for dunking chips.

Preparation 20 minutes
Makes enough for 4

2 egg yolks
2 teaspoons Dijon mustard
1 teaspoon English mustard
2 teaspoons white wine vinegar
1 garlic clove, crushed to a paste
300 ml olive oil
sea salt and freshly ground black pepper

Put the egg yolks, mustards, vinegar and garlic in a bowl and mix well. Season, add a drop of oil and mix again. Continue adding the oil a drop at a time, mixing after each addition; this will prevent the mayo curdling. Adjust the seasoning if necessary. Store in the fridge until needed.

hollandaise sauce

This is traditionally served with fish and steamed vegetables.

Preparation 20 minutes
Makes enough for 4

250 g butter
2 egg yolks
1 tablespoon white wine vinegar
sea salt and fine white pepper

Melt the butter in a small saucepan. Put the egg yolks in a small heatproof jug and whisk with a hand-held blender. Continue blending very slowly as you pour in the butter so that the mixture emulsifies. Add the vinegar and seasoning, and blend again. Put clingfilm directly on top of the sauce to prevent a skin forming. Place the jug in a saucepan of hot water for 10 minutes, or until needed.

harissa

Use this spicy Moroccan sauce with couscous or roast meats.

Preparation 30 minutes
Cooking 1 hour
Makes enough for 4

150 ml olive oil
2 red onions, chopped
5 garlic cloves, crushed
1 teaspoon ground cumin seeds
1 teaspoon ground fennel seeds
1 teaspoon ground coriander seeds
3 roasted red peppers, peeled, deseeded and chopped
6 medium-hot red chillies, deseeded and chopped

Heat the oil in a pan and gently sauté the onions and garlic without colouring for 10 minutes. Add the seeds and cook for a few minutes. Stir in the peppers and chillies and simmer for 10 minutes. Transfer to a blender or food processor and blitz until smooth. Return to the pan and cook very slowly for a further 30 minutes. Remove and let cool. Store in the fridge, topped with olive oil, for up to 3 weeks.

charmoula

A Middle Eastern sauce served with grilled fish and meat.

Preparation 25 minutes + 1 hour steeping
Makes enough for 4

4 tablespoons olive oil
2 tablespoons wine vinegar
2 tablespoons runny honey
2 garlic cloves, crushed
1 red chilli, finely diced
2 teaspoons cumin
2 teaspoons paprika
a bunch of flat leaf parsley, finely chopped
5 spring onions, thinly sliced
50 g raisins
250 g carrots, finely grated
sea salt and freshly ground black pepper

Combine the olive oil, vinegar and honey in a bowl, then stir in the garlic, chilli, cumin and paprika. Add the parsley, spring onions, raisins and carrots, season and mix well, then let stand for 1 hour before serving.

chilli sauce

A medium-hot sauce that will add a kick to all savoury dishes.

Preparation 10 minutes
Cooking 30 minutes
Makes enough for 4

4 garlic cloves, crushed
4 red chillies, chopped
100 g sugar

Put the garlic and chillies in a small pan, cover with 200 ml water and bring to a simmer. Cook for 30 minutes, checking the water level frequently and adding more if needed. Remove from the heat and stir in the sugar. Blitz with a hand-held blender until smooth and let cool before using.

green sauce

The vibrant colour of this sauce comes from the herbs it contains. It is often used on pasta, and is also good with barbecued meats and fish.

Preparation 30 minutes
Makes enough for 4

a bunch of parsley, finely chopped
a bunch of coriander, finely chopped
a bunch of dill, finely chopped
a bunch of watercress, chopped
1 tablespoon capers, finely chopped
2 garlic cloves, crushed
100 ml olive oil
sea salt and freshly ground black pepper

Put all the herbs in a bowl with the watercress, capers and garlic, and mix well. Drizzle in the olive oil, season and mix again.

gremolata

An Italian sauce that usually accompanies *osso bucco* (stewed shin of veal), but it also goes well with lamb and other meats.

Preparation 10 minutes
Makes enough for 4

3 garlic cloves, finely chopped
a large bunch of parsley, finely chopped
zest and juice of 2 unwaxed lemons
100 ml olive oil
sea salt and freshly ground black pepper

Put all the ingredients in a bowl and mix well. The texture should be fine. In fact, the more finely chopped the ingredients, the better the sauce.

tartare sauce

A mayonnaise-type sauce usually served with fish. Why not try it with chips or jacket potatoes too?

Preparation 20 minutes
Makes enough for 4

2 egg yolks
½ teaspoon English mustard powder
200 ml olive oil
juice of 1 lemon
1 tablespoon capers, chopped
1 tablespoon gherkins, chopped
1 shallot, chopped
1 tablespoon parsley, chopped
sea salt and freshly ground black pepper

Put the egg and mustard powder in a bowl and whisk together. Drizzle in the olive oil very slowly, whisking constantly. Add the lemon juice and mix well. Stir in the capers, gherkins, shallot and parsley, season and mix again. Refrigerate if not using straight away.

hot and sour sauce

This exotic sauce is a good dip for prawns and chicken, and can also be used to dress an Asian salad.

Preparation 20 minutes
Cooking 30 minutes
Makes enough for 4

6 medium-sized green chillies, deseeded and chopped
juice of 4 limes
10 cm galangal or fresh ginger, peeled and chopped
a pinch of sea salt

Put the chillies in a small saucepan, add the lime juice, galangal and salt, add just enough water to cover and bring to a simmer. Bubble gentle for 30 minutes, adding more water if needed.

Blitz with a hand-held blender to make a smoothish sauce. Taste and adjust the seasoning and consistency, by adding a little more water, if you wish.

sweet treats

We hear a lot about the incidence of obesity these days and that's something we certainly don't want to contribute to. None of us wants to be fat, or cause our loved ones to gain an unhealthy amount of weight. But that doesn't mean we can't have the occasional sweet treat. As with most things in life, moderation is the watchword.

This section starts with cakes and cookies, which most people can enjoy with a clear conscience from time to time. I've tried to maximize the healthy ingredients in them, using unrefined products whenever possible. This means that they release their energy slowly rather than giving an instant rush that can lead to craving more and more sugar.

The puddings follow similar principles, aiming to combine the best ingredients with the most delicious flavours. Your family will love them all!

classic flapjacks

A healthy and sustaining snack
that keeps you going for hours.

Preparation 10 minutes
Cooking 20 minutes
Makes 8

200 g butter
1 tablespoon golden syrup
200 g soft brown sugar
250 g rolled oats

*a shallow baking tin, 20 x 30 cm, lined with
baking parchment*

Preheat the oven to 150ºC (300ºF) Gas 2.

Melt the butter in a large saucepan, add
the syrup and sugar and stir until the
sugar has dissolved. Remove from the
heat and stir in the oats. Spoon the
mixture into the prepared baking tin and
bake for 20 minutes. When done, cut
into squares straight away and let cool.

honeyjacks

You can use any type of honey
in this recipe because they all
become runny when heated.

Preparation 10 minutes
Cooking 20 minutes
Makes 8

200g butter
1 tablespoon golden syrup
125g soft brown sugar
75g honey
200g rolled oats
50g raisins
100 g desiccated coconut

*a shallow baking tin, 20 x 30 cm, lined with
baking parchment*

Preheat the oven to 150ºC (300ºF) Gas 2.
Melt the butter in a large saucepan, add
the syrup, sugar and honey, then stir
until the sugar has dissolved. Remove
from the heat and stir in the oats and
raisins. Spoon the mixture into the
prepared baking tin, sprinkle with the
coconut and bake for 20 minutes.

When done, cut into squares straight
away and let cool before eating.

nutty jacks

Nuts are high in protein and fibre,
so they make a healthy addition
to flapjacks.

Preparation 10 minutes
Cooking 20 minutes
Makes 8

200 g butter
1 tablespoon golden syrup
200 g soft brown sugar
200 g rolled oats
50 g chopped nuts
100–200 g good-quality
dark chocolate, melted

*a shallow baking tin, 20 x 30 cm, lined with
baking parchment*

Preheat the oven to 150ºC (300ºF) Gas 2.

Melt the butter in a large saucepan, add
the syrup and sugar and stir until the
sugar has dissolved. Remove from the
heat and stir in the oats and nuts.
Spoon the mixture into the prepared
baking tin, place in the oven and bake
for 20 minutes.

When done, cut into squares
immediately and let cool. Drizzle the
melted chocolate over the nutty jacks
in a zigzag pattern and allow to set
before eating.

oat and chocolate cookies

My friend Rebecca, who loves to cook, gave me the recipe for these much-loved biscuits. They're a staple treat in my family.

Preparation 20 minutes
Cooking 20 minutes
Makes 15–20

250 g butter, softened
50 g unrefined caster sugar
115 g light brown sugar
115 g plain chocolate drops
175 g oats
200 g self-raising flour

Preheat the oven to 180°C (350°F) Gas 4.

Cream together the butter and sugars. Stir in the chocolate drops and oats. Add the flour and mix well.

Using your hands, form the mixture into 15–20 small balls. Flatten them slightly with your palms and place them on a baking sheet, allowing room for growth. Bake in the oven for 15–20 minutes.

When done, cool on a wire rack and store in an airtight tin.

shortbread

A classic three-ingredient biscuit, ideal for children to help make. Take care that the flour is not overmixed or the finished dough will be tough.

Preparation 15 minutes
Cooking 45 minutes
Makes 16

200 g butter, softened
100 g unrefined caster sugar, plus extra for sprinkling
300 g plain flour

a loose-bottomed baking tin, 20 cm square, lightly buttered

Preheat the oven to 150°C (300°F) Gas 2.

Cream the butter and sugar together until light and smooth. Add the flour and mix quickly with the back of a wooden spoon until the mixture resembles breadcrumbs.

Tip the mixture into the prepared baking tin. Flatten evenly with the back of a spoon and sprinkle with a little extra sugar. Bake for 45 minutes.

When done, remove from the oven and let cool for about 5 minutes, before cutting into 16 squares. Store in an airtight container.

pumpkin seed cookies

Seeds contain lots of nutrients that are an important part of a good diet. A great way to feed them to your family is to hide them in cookies, and these ones are really quick and easy to make.

Preparation 20 minutes
Cooking 12–15 minutes
Makes 20

200 g self-raising flour
125 g butter, diced
125 g light muscovado sugar
1 egg, beaten
75 g pumpkin seeds

Preheat the oven to 180°C (350°F) Gas 4.

Put the flour, butter and sugar in a bowl and mix with a fork until the mixure resembles breadcrumbs. Add the egg and seeds, mix again and form into a ball. Lightly flour a work surface and use your hands to roll the dough into a sausage shape about 20 cm long. Cut into 20 slices and place on a non-stick or buttered baking sheet. Bake for 12–15 minutes.

When done, cool on a wire rack, then store in an airtight container.

basic cake

Preparation 45 minutes
Cooking 35–45 minutes

300 g margarine
300 g unrefined caster sugar
5 eggs
1 teaspoon vanilla extract
350 g self-raising flour
1 teaspoon baking powder
Icing
200 g icing sugar
juice of 1 lemon

a shallow baking tin, 20 x 30 cm, lined with baking parchment

This light, moist sponge cake can be dressed up or down to suit any family occasion.

Preheat the oven to 180°C (350°F) Gas 4. Put the margarine and caster sugar in a bowl and mix until light and fluffy. Beat in the eggs, then stir in the vanilla extract. Sift in the flour and baking powder, then fold together quickly with a large spoon (speed at this stage keeps the cake light). Spoon the mixture into the prepared baking tin, place in the middle of the oven and bake for 30–35 minutes. When done, a knife inserted in the centre of the cake should come out clean; if it doesn't, cook for a further 5–10 minutes. Cool in the tin for 5 minutes, then turn out onto a wire rack and let cool completely.

To make the icing, sift the sugar into a bowl and stir in the lemon juice. Carefully add a little water to make a smooth, stiff paste. Place the cake on a plate and use a wet palette knife to spread the icing over the top. Decorate with sweets or berries if you wish, then allow to set before serving.

lemon polenta cake

Preparation 20 minutes
Cooking 30 minutes

175 g butter, softened
175 g unrefined caster sugar
100 g polenta
½ teaspoon baking powder
175 g ground almonds
zest and juice of 1 unwaxed lemon
½ teaspoon vanilla extract
3 eggs
Syrup
zest and juice of 2 unwaxed lemons
50 g unrefined caster sugar

a springform cake tin, 24 cm in diameter, lightly greased

Polenta, or cornmeal, gives a slighter coarser texture than wheat flour, but is still delicious.

Preheat the oven to 180°C (350°F) Gas 4. Beat together the butter and sugar until creamy. Add the polenta, baking powder, ground almonds, lemon zest and juice, vanilla extract and eggs. Mix together until smooth. Spoon the mixture into the prepared tin and bake in the middle of the oven for 30 minutes.

Meanwhile, make the syrup. Put the lemon zest and juice in a small saucepan with the icing sugar and 2 tablespoons of water. Bring to the boil and simmer for 2 minutes. When the cake is done, let cool slightly in the tin, then turn out and pierce all over with a fine skewer. Spoon the syrup over the cake, then let stand for 20 minutes while it is absorbed. Serve with crème fraîche.

devil's food cake

Preparation 30 minutes
Cooking 20 minutes

100 g butter
100 g soft, light brown sugar
100 g golden syrup
150 g plain flour
30 g cocoa powder
1 egg, beaten
1 teaspoon bicarbonate of soda
150 ml milk
Frosting
3 tablespoons cocoa powder
3 tablespoons hot water
100 g butter, softened
200 g icing sugar
1 tablespoon golden syrup
2 drops vanilla extract

*2 sandwich tins, 18 cm in diameter,
greased*

Wickedly rich and chocolatey, this cake will have everyone clamouring for more.

Preheat the oven to 180°C (350°F) Gas 4.

Put the butter, sugar and golden syrup in a saucepan and heat gently until the sugar has dissolved.

Sift the flour and cocoa into a bowl, add the sugar mixture and stir well. Add the egg and mix again. Combine the bicarbonate of soda with the milk, add to the bowl and mix thoroughly. Divide the mixture between the prepared cake tins and smooth out with a palette knife. Place in the oven and cook for 20 minutes, until just firm to the touch. Turn onto a wire rack to cool.

To make the frosting, put the cocoa in a bowl and mix in the hot water. Add the butter, sugar, golden syrup and vanilla extract and beat until smooth.

When the cakes are cold, sandwich together with some of the frosting. (Dip your palette knife in hot water to prevent the frosting sticking to it.) Spread the remainder over the top and sides of the cake, making the surface as smooth or ruffled as you wish.

carrot cake

Preparation 30 minutes
Cooking 1 hour

4 eggs, separated
240 g soft brown sugar
zest and juice of 1 unwaxed orange
240 g ground walnuts
1 teaspoon cinnamon
250 g carrot, grated
100 g wholemeal flour
1 teaspoon baking powder
Frosting
200 g cream cheese
100 g icing sugar
zest and juice of 1 small orange

*a loose-bottomed cake tin,
20 cm square, greased*

A scrumptious teatime treat – no wonder it's also known as 'passion cake'!

Preheat the oven to 180°C (350°F) Gas 4.

Put the egg yolks and sugar in a bowl and whisk until thick and creamy. Add all the remaining ingredients, except the egg white, and fold carefully until the mixture is smooth.

Whisk the egg whites until stiff, then fold into the cake mixture. Pour into the prepared cake tin and bake in the centre of the oven for 1 hour. When done, cool in the tin for 5 minutes, then turn out and cool completely on a wire rack.

To make the frosting, cream the cheese and icing sugar together. Add a little orange zest and juice to flavour. Spread over the top of the cold cake using a palette knife dipped in hot water. Sprinkle with the remaining orange zest.

banana cake

Preparation 20 minutes
Cooking 1 hour

175 g golden caster sugar
1 tablespoon golden syrup
200 ml vegetable oil
2 eggs
2 ripe bananas
1 teaspoon vanilla extract
300 g self-raising flour
1 teaspoon baking powder

a 1-kg loaf tin, lightly greased

In my family this cake is popular even with those who don't like bananas. The flavour improves with keeping, so wrap the cake in clingfilm and keep for a couple of days before cutting.

Preheat the oven to 180°C (350°F) Gas 4.

Put the sugar and golden syrup in a bowl. Put the oil, eggs, bananas and vanilla extract in another bowl and whiz with a hand-held blender. Add to the bowl of sugar and mix until smooth. Fold in the flour and baking powder, then spoon into the prepared tin. Bake in the middle of the oven for 50–60 minutes. When it is done, a knife inserted in the centre of the cake should come out clean.

seasonal fruit tray tart

Preparation 30 minutes
Cooking 45 minutes
Serves 6

500 g puff pastry
1 kg seasonal fruit, such as apples, apricots, nectarines, peaches or plums, cored or stoned, as necessary
1 egg, beaten
50 g unrefined caster sugar
50 g butter
runny honey, for drizzling
icing sugar, for dusting

A simple dessert that makes the most of any fruit in season. Serve with whipped cream or crème fraîche for a special treat.

Preheat the oven to 180°C (350°F) Gas 4. Lightly grease a baking sheet.

Dust a work surface with flour and roll out the pastry to approximately 30 x 30 cm. Lay the pastry out on the prepared baking sheet. Arrange the fruit on the pastry in an even layer, leaving a 4-cm border around the edges. Brush the border with the egg and fold inwards all the way around. Sprinkle the fruit with the caster sugar and dot with the butter.

Bake for 45 minutes, reducing the heat if the pastry shows signs of burning. Drizzle with honey and dust with icing sugar before serving.

chocolate swamp pudding

Preparation 30 minutes
Cooking 25 minutes
Serves 4

100 g butter
125 g unrefined caster sugar
125 ml milk
2 eggs
1 teaspoon vanilla extract
125 g self-raising flour
60 g cocoa powder
Chocolate swamp
180 g soft brown sugar
30 g cocoa powder
250 ml boiling water

a 1-litre ovenproof dish, buttered

Melt-in-the-mouth chocolate sponge floating in chocolate sauce – this is a pudding to die for.

Preheat the oven to 180°C (350°F) Gas 4.

Put the butter, sugar and milk in a saucepan and heat gently until the sugar has dissolved. Set aside to cool.

Whisk the eggs in a bowl and add the vanilla extract. Sift the flour and cocoa into a large bowl, add the milk and the egg mixture and stir until smooth. Pour into the prepared baking dish and set aside.

To make the chocolate swamp, mix the sugar and cocoa powder together, then sprinkle evenly over the top of the pudding. Pour on the boiling water and bake in the oven for 25 minutes.

almond fruit crumble

Preparation 30 minutes
Cooking 30 minutes
Serves 4

600 g fruit
50 g light brown sugar
125 g self-raising flour
1 teaspoon baking powder
125 g butter, diced
50 g unrefined caster sugar
50 g ground almonds
50 g rolled oats

a 1-litre ovenproof dish, buttered

You can't go wrong with a crumble, and the fruit variations are endless. Try rhubarb and ginger, apple and apricot, pear and blackcurrant or whatever's in the fruit bowl.

Preheat the oven to 190°C (375°F) Gas 5. Put the fruit in the prepared dish, add the brown sugar and 100 ml water.

Put the flour, baking powder and butter in a bowl and rub together with your fingertips until the mixture resembles breadcrumbs. Stir in the caster sugar, almonds and oats, then spoon evenly over the fruit. Bake in the oven for 30 minutes. The crumble should be golden and the fruit bubbling up around the edges. Serve with custard, cream or ice cream.

apple and blackberry pie

Preparation 45 minutes
Cooking 40 minutes
Serves 6

250 g plain flour
175 g butter, diced
80 g unrefined caster sugar
2 eggs, beaten
Filling
1 kg apples, peeled and cored
400 g blackberries
100 g unrefined caster sugar

a loose-bottomed flan case, 25 cm in diameter, lightly buttered

An old favourite that every family should have in its culinary repertoire.

Preheat the oven to 180°C (350°F) Gas 4. Put the flour and butter in a bowl and rub together with your fingertips until the mixture resembles breadcrumbs. Stir in the sugar, then add all but 2 tablespoons of the eggs and mix to form a dough. Set aside one-third of the pastry.

Lightly flour a work surface, roll out the larger piece of dough and use to line the flan case. Mix the apples, blackberries and sugar in a bowl and put inside the lined flan case.

Roll out the smaller piece of dough a little larger than the flan case. Brush the inside edge of the pastry base with a little of the remaining egg and put the pastry sheet on top of the fruit. Pinch the edges together to seal. Brush the top with the remaining beaten egg, sprinkle with a little sugar and bake in the oven for 40 minutes, until golden.

upside-down fruit pudding

Preparation 30 minutes

Cooking 25 minutes

Serves 6

3 pears, peeled, cored and halved

100 g butter, softened

100 g unrefined caster sugar

40 g ground almonds

2 eggs

100 g self-raising flour

30 g cocoa powder

1 teaspoon baking powder

75 ml milk

icing sugar, for dusting

a loose-bottomed flan tin, 25 cm in diameter, buttered

A sophisticated-looking pudding that is really easy to make. Any fresh, ripe fruit can be used, but pears are particularly good.

Preheat the oven to 180°C (350°F) Gas 4. Arrange the pears in the bottom of the flan tin. Put the butter and sugar in a bowl and cream until smooth. Add the ground almonds and eggs and beat well. Sift in the flour, cocoa and baking powder, then fold the mixture together. Add the milk and mix until smooth. Cover the pears with the mixture, smoothing it out with a palette knife. Bake for 25 minutes.

When done, let cool for 10 minutes, then invert onto a plate. Remove the outer ring of the flan case, and lift off the base by sliding a palette knife underneath it. Dust the pudding with icing sugar and serve with clotted cream.

steamed lemon and blueberry pudding

Preparation 25 minutes

Cooking 45 minutes

Serves 6

300 g blueberries, fresh or frozen (no need to thaw)

120 g butter, softened

120 g unrefined caster sugar

2 eggs

zest and juice of 2 unwaxed lemons

175 g self-raising flour

1 teaspoon baking powder

a 1.5-litre pudding basin, buttered and dusted with caster sugar

The combination of blueberries and lemon is heavenly: try it and see.

Put the blueberries in the prepared pudding basin. Cream the butter and sugar together, add the eggs and beat well. Stir in the lemon juice and zest. Sift in the flour and baking powder and fold into the mixture. Spoon on top of the blueberries and level with the back of a spoon. Cover with a sheet of foil or baking parchment and secure with a rubber band or string.

Quarter fill a large saucepan with hot water, place the pudding bowl in it, then cover and simmer for 45 minutes. Check from time to time, adding more water if necessary. When done, remove the bowl and ease a palette knife around the pudding. Invert onto a serving plate, give it a litle shake, then lift off the basin. Serve with crème fraîche.

french pancakes

It's great fun (and less work for you) to set up a 'pancake bar' on the kitchen table and let all the family members help themselves to their favourite topping (see right).

Preparation 15 minutes + 30 minutes chilling
Cooking 10 minutes
Makes 12

100 g plain flour
300 ml milk
1 large free-range egg
a little butter or vegetable oil, for frying

Put the flour, milk and egg in a blender or food processor and whiz until smooth. Transfer the mixture to a jug, cover and chill for 30 minutes. (The batter can be made in advance and kept for up to 24 hours.)

Wipe a frying pan with the butter and heat. Add a ladleful of batter, tilting the pan to spread it evenly. Cook for 1–2 minutes on each side until light brown. Stack the pancakes on a large plate and keep warm. To serve, fold or roll up a pancake and add the topping of your choice.

pancake toppings

The simplest ideas are often the best, so here are some quick and easy toppings.

Quick chocolate sauce

150 g good-quality plain chocolate
2 tablespoons golden syrup
70 g unsalted butter
1 tablespoon brandy (optional)

Put all the ingredients in a small saucepan and melt over a low heat, stirring continuously until smooth.

Lemon and sugar
The classic way of serving pancakes: squeeze some lemon over the top and sprinkle with a little caster sugar.

Honey and walnuts
Offer a pot of runny honey with a drizzler and a little dish of chopped walnuts for scattering.

Fruit jam and crème fraîche
Spread good-quality raspberry or strawberry jam on the pancake and top generously with chilled crème fraîche.

meringues with baked plums

Preparation 10 minutes
Cooking 1–4 hours
Makes 4–6

3 egg whites
225 g unrefined caster sugar
16 plums
1 cinnamon stick

a small ovenproof dish with a lid

They look impressive, but meringues are easy to make and the family will love them.

Preheat the oven to 140°C (275°F) Gas 1. Line a baking sheet with baking parchment. Whisk the egg whites until stiff. Add 175 g sugar and whisk until smooth. Place 8 spoonfuls of the mixture on the parchment, spacing them well apart. Bake in the middle of the oven for 1 hour if you like your meringues to have a soft centre, or up to 4 hours if you prefer them dry.

Put the plums, cinnamon and the remaining sugar in the prepared dish, add 50 ml water and bake in the oven with the meringues for 1 hour. Serve together, topped with yoghurt.

lemon meringue pie

Preparation 45 minutes
Cooking 45 minutes
Serves 6

zest and juice of 3 unwaxed lemons
300 g unrefined caster sugar
60 g butter
40 g cornflour
3 eggs, separated
Pastry
250 g plain flour
125 g butter, diced
30 g unrefined caster sugar
2 eggs, beaten

a loose-bottomed flan tin, 20 cm in diameter, lightly buttered

Crumbly pastry, tangy lemon and fluffy meringue – the perfect family pudding!

First make the pastry. Put the flour and butter in a bowl and rub together with your fingertips until the mixture resembles breadcrumbs. Add the caster sugar, then pour in the eggs and mix until you have a dough.

Preheat the oven to 180°C (350°F) Gas 4. Flour a work surface, roll out the dough and use to line the prepared flan tin. Line the pastry case with baking parchment and fill with baking beans. Bake for 25 minutes. Remove the parchment and beans. Lower the heat to 150°C (300°F) Gas 2 and bake for a further 20 minutes.

To make the filling, put the lemon zest and juice in a saucepan, add 125 g of the sugar plus the butter and cornflour, and heat gently, stirring constantly until thick. Take off the heat and cool for 10 minutes. Beat in the egg yolks.

For the meringue, whisk the egg whites until stiff, then whisk in the remaining sugar. Spoon the lemon filling into the pastry case, top with the meringue and bake for 15 minutes.